THE WORLD OF

History
Revision

James Dixon

Contents

Dr Malthus's mistake

Dr Malthus was a vicar and schoolteacher. In 1798, he calculated that populations rise geometrically (2, 4, 8, 16, etc.) whereas food and resources increase arithmetically (2, 4, 6, 8, etc.). He predicted that the population was rising too quickly and that Britain would soon have too many mouths to feed. Like many teachers, Malthus was wrong! He did not foresee the great innovations of the Industrial Revolution.

Between 1750 and 1900 the population of Britain did increase, from less than 10 million to more than 40 million. In 1900, the number of people in England alone was six times greater than it had been 200 years before.

We cannot be certain of the exact number of people in Britain between 1750 and 1900. However, every ten years since 1801 the government has carried out a <u>census</u>. By 1900, this was very accurate in showing who lived in Britain, and recording other details, such as their jobs.

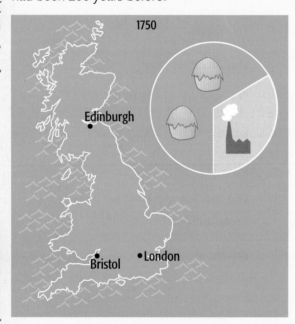

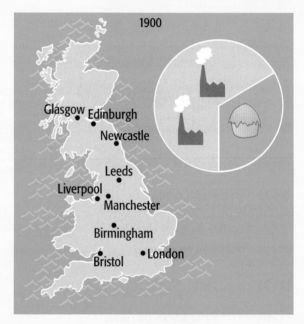

At the same time, more people started to live in the big towns and cities. In 1750, about a third of the British population lived in towns and cities.

In 1900, about two thirds of the population lived in towns and cities. Many people born in the countryside were suddenly attracted to towns by the opportunity of getting work in the new industries and factories there. However, there was also a significant rise in poverty at this time.

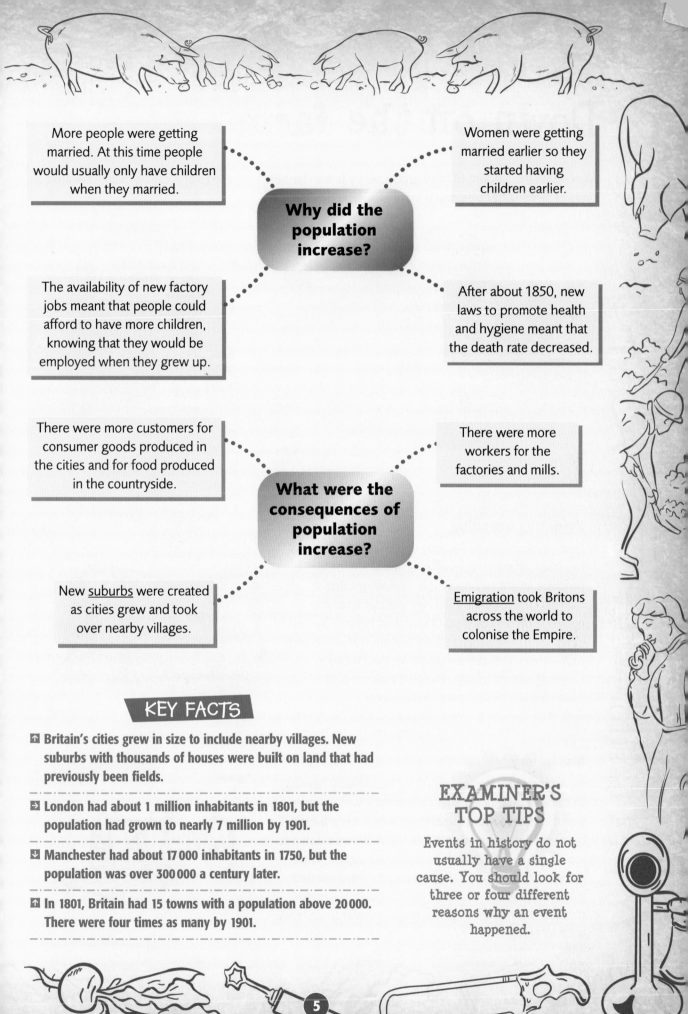

More people were getting married. At this time people would usually only have children when they married.

Women were getting married earlier so they started having children earlier.

Why did the population increase?

The availability of new factory jobs meant that people could afford to have more children, knowing that they would be employed when they grew up.

After about 1850, new laws to promote health and hygiene meant that the death rate decreased.

There were more customers for consumer goods produced in the cities and for food produced in the countryside.

There were more workers for the factories and mills.

What were the consequences of population increase?

New <u>suburbs</u> were created as cities grew and took over nearby villages.

<u>Emigration</u> took Britons across the world to colonise the Empire.

KEY FACTS

⬆ Britain's cities grew in size to include nearby villages. New suburbs with thousands of houses were built on land that had previously been fields.

➋ London had about 1 million inhabitants in 1801, but the population had grown to nearly 7 million by 1901.

⬇ Manchester had about 17 000 inhabitants in 1750, but the population was over 300 000 a century later.

⬆ In 1801, Britain had 15 towns with a population above 20 000. There were four times as many by 1901.

EXAMINER'S TOP TIPS

Events in history do not usually have a single cause. You should look for three or four different reasons why an event happened.

Down on the farm

After 1650, the amount of food produced by British farmers increased significantly, mainly because all kinds of farming became much more efficient.

Selective breeding

Farmers discovered that they could selectively breed together different types of a particular animal to produce an entirely new type. This meant that animals kept for their meat, like pigs for example, could be bred to be much fatter than before. Some cows were bred so that they were good at producing milk, others so that they would be ideal for beef. Growing turnips as part of crop rotation meant more animals could be fed even in the winter.

Machinery

New machinery was an important reason why farming became more efficient. The Industrial Revolution meant that there were more metal tools, which were better than wooden ones. From 1750, horse-drawn machines – such as this seed-drill for sowing the seed in fields – made many jobs faster. Fewer workers were needed than before. From 1850, the use of 'traction engines' (tractors with steam engines) made it easier to do tasks such as ploughing.

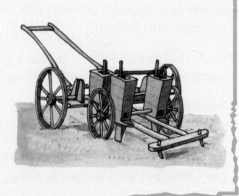

Enclosure

In medieval times, farmland in each village was divided up into a few big open fields, and the villagers owned several strips in each field. By 1801, many villages had 'enclosed' these fields – dividing them up amongst the most important villagers who then built walls or planted hedgerows around their new farms.

In 1801, the enclosure of the entire British countryside became law when Parliament passed the General Enclosure Acts. This was more efficient as it meant that each farmer could concentrate on just his own piece of land. He could also improve it as much as he wanted to, without having to get his neighbours to agree.

More land was available for cultivation when marsh or <u>fenland</u> was drained in eastern England.

Crop rotation

Farmers learned new crop rotation methods to keep the soil in their fields productive. In particular, they could use different types of crops at different times of the year, so the land was never just left <u>fallow</u>. They also learned to use clay and lime fertilisers instead of just animal manure.

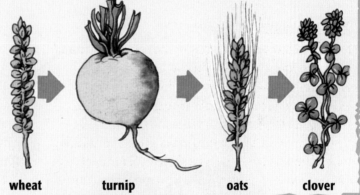

wheat **turnip** **oats** **clover**

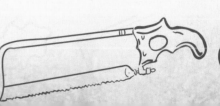

Made in Britain

In the 19th century, Britain was the world leader for producing the goods shown on these pages. They were exported around the world and the industries that produced them employed many thousands of people. Furthermore, these were among the most important industries at the heart of the Industrial Revolution, which began in Britain before anywhere else.

Coal

Coal was essential as the fuel for steam-powered trains and ships. It powered the machines in the mills and factories and was needed for making coke (used in making iron and steel). Coal became the main fuel for heating homes. Thanks to the positive cycle shown below, production increased rapidly:

- 1783 – 6 million tons
- 1815 – 15 million tons
- 1855 – 65 million tons

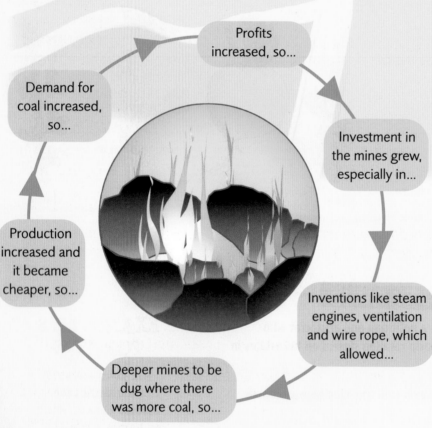

Profits increased, so...

Demand for coal increased, so...

Investment in the mines grew, especially in...

Production increased and it became cheaper, so...

Inventions like steam engines, ventilation and wire rope, which allowed...

Deeper mines to be dug where there was more coal, so...

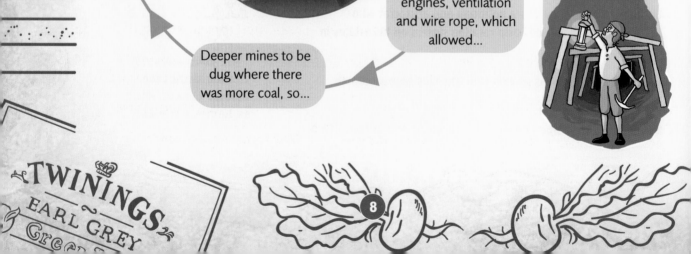

Cotton

Colonies in India and the West Indies grew the plant from which cotton thread is made just for Britain. Even more cotton was available from America as production there rose after it became independent in 1783.

Colonies in India, the West Indies and also America after 1783 supplied large quantities of raw cotton to Britain.

Cheaper clothes were manufactured due to new inventions. New machines were initially used by individual spinners and weavers at home, then in huge factories.

Lancashire = the 'Cotton King'

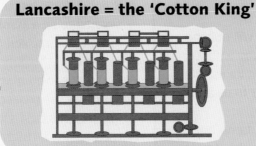

Customer demand for cotton clothes rose as the population in Britain and the Empire increased.

Counties like Lancashire had the right sort of damp climate to preserve the cotton yarn, with many rivers to provide water power. They were also close to coal mines when steam power replaced water power.

Control of the seas by the Royal Navy meant Britain could easily export its goods to customers anywhere in the world.

Cotton inventors and inventions:

* James Hargreaves invented the Spinning Jenny.
* Richard Arkwright invented the water frame.
* Samuel Crompton invented the Spinning Mule.

Iron and steel

EXAMINER'S TOP TIPS

Historical revolutions are times of change that affect many people in society, change many aspects of their lives and occur relatively quickly.

Britain was at the centre of improvements in the technology for making iron during the 18th century, and for making steel cheaply in the 19th century. Sheffield stainless steel was the best in the world.

KEY FACTS

Date	Inventor	Invention	Improvement
1709	Abraham Darby	Used coke to make cast iron	Coke was cheaper than charcoal
1784	Henry Cort	Process for making wrought iron in factories or 'mills'	Cheaper than making it by hand, wrought iron is stronger than cast iron
1828	John Neilson	Hot-blast system	Halved the amount of coal needed
1856	Henry Bessemer	Process for making steel	Steel now cheap and easily made

Full steam ahead

THE LIVERPOOL AND MANCHESTER RAILWAY COMPANY

Calling all Engineers, Inventors and Mechanics!

Can you design and build a Locomotive Machine that will pull the carriages on our new railway without horses? If you have what it takes, bring your vehicle to the Rainhill Trials and let us put it to the test.

The winner will receive fame and money – he will even have his face printed on £5 notes!

A once in a lifetime chance… No time-wasters!

TRAIN TRAGEDY

From our transport correspondent Polly Perkins, September 1830

Following last year's run-away victory at the Rainhill Trials, Mr Stephenson's locomotive The Rocket seemed to be a symbol of progress, although some scientists predicted that travelling at its amazing top speed of 28 miles per hour would actually suffocate the passengers.

Sadly, the first victim of high-speed travel came straight after yesterday's opening of the Liverpool and Manchester Railway, when a dazed and confused passenger, the politician William Huskisson MP, was run over and killed.

Key people

Isambard Kingdom Brunel was the great engineer and businessman responsible for building the Great Western Railway, started in 1835, including its tunnels and bridges, and even the hotels for travellers. He also built the Great Eastern passenger liner in 1858.

George Stephenson built the Stockton and Darlington railway in 1825 and The Rocket locomotive in 1829.

Thomas Telford built canals, bridges and roads in the early 19th century, including the London to Holyhead road for passengers heading to Ireland.

For or against canals?

Barges were able to carry large quantities of goods like coal.

Once the canal was dug it became very cheap to transport coal.

By 1800 the canal system stretched across most of England.

Barges were very slow so they were less useful for transporting food or people.

Canals were only a cheap form of transport for very bulky items or large quantities.

For

Against

How did Britain's roads improve?

- <u>Turnpike</u> Trusts were set up by local people. These trusts charged road users a toll and used the money to repair the road.

- The methods and materials used for making and repairing roads improved.

- The design of horse-drawn coaches changed, making them faster and more comfortable for travellers.

Why were the railways so important?

- Trains were much faster than any other form of transport.

- They could carry people and all types of goods, from post or newspapers to coal or steel.

- They employed thousands of people, first to build the railways and then to run them.

- They used huge quantities of steel, coal and other products, which boosted these industries.

- They made British goods much cheaper and easier to transport than goods manufactured abroad.

- They helped the British to become the leading and most prosperous industrial economy.

- They connected every part of Britain in a single transport network.

EXAMINER'S TOP TIPS

A source may be more useful if it contains factual information, such as names or dates.

11

Tea and coffee

In the 18th and 19th centuries, Britain became the greatest trading nation in the world. It was the centre for industries like ship-building. It was the biggest importer of raw cotton and the biggest exporter of cotton clothes and other manufactured goods. London became the heart of the world's financial system.

Transport became faster and cheaper due to the sail-powered tea clippers and then later the steam ships.

Royal Navy ships could protect British merchants and their ships almost anywhere.

Affordable mass-produced consumer goods produced in British factories were popular all over the world.

Domination of many industries meant that Britain was often the best or only supplier of some goods.

Empire stretching right around the globe meant that Britain had colonies to provide it with almost all its imports and markets for many of its exports.

The Anti-Corn Law League

From 1815 several Corn Laws were passed. They banned the import of wheat from abroad so people in Britain could only buy the wheat grown in this country. The aim of the laws was to protect the income of farmers, but it also meant the price of bread always stayed high. The Anti-Corn Law League was founded in 1839 to campaign to <u>repeal</u> these laws so that ordinary people would be able to buy cheap food. The laws were repealed in 1846 and Britain allowed free trade in food. This period in history has become known as the 'hungry forties'.

TWININGS
EARL GREY

The City of London and the Commercial Revolution

In the 18th century, London's merchants met in coffee houses in the narrow streets of the City of London. This is where they discussed business, agreed contracts and planned future voyages. By 1900 the Bank of England, Lloyds Insurers, the Stock Exchange and many other London banks and organisations dominated the world's financial system.

London was the international centre for:

- banking and lending money
- insurance for businesses and shipping
- stocks and shares.

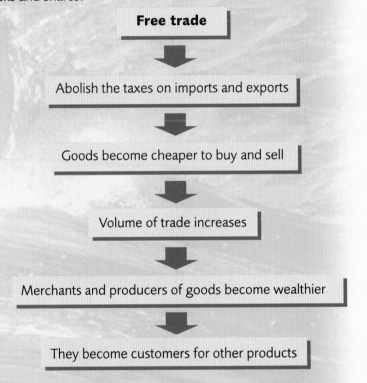

Free trade

⬇

Abolish the taxes on imports and exports

⬇

Goods become cheaper to buy and sell

⬇

Volume of trade increases

⬇

Merchants and producers of goods become wealthier

⬇

They become customers for other products

EXAMINER'S TOP TIPS

Some historical events are due to a single important man or woman, but other events are more to do with the actions of many ordinary people.

KEY FACTS

▶ Adam Smith promoted the idea of free trade in his book, *The Wealth of Nations*, published in 1776.

▶ Thomas Twining was one of the men who made a fortune from selling tea.

▶ Richard Cobden and John Bright led the successful campaign against the Corn Laws.

▶ Samuel Smiles published his book, *Self Help,* in 1859. He advised people to take responsibility for their own life and criticised those who rely on the government or other people.

The great metropolis

Historical records show that London has always had an unpleasant smell about it, but in 1858 the Great Stink was so unbearable that even MPs in Westminster noticed it. The problem was that the sewers were too small and simply emptied everything into the River Thames.

Sewage solutions

'Let's transport the filth away in railway carriages.' Mr W Smith

'We could change the direction of the Thames.' Rev Moses Jones

'We must open more public lavatories!' Sir Walter Close

'I say we should recycle it!' Mr A Steptoe

'Just pour perfume into the river.' Miss E Lauder

'Why don't we cover over the river with concrete?' Mrs S C Portland

The actual solution was a vast network of tunnels and sewers built by Sir Joseph Bazalgette. It used 318 mm bricks over 1100 miles in a system that is still in use today.

The story of London's sewers is just one example of how our Victorian ancestors came up with new ways to deal with the various problems caused by running the biggest city that had ever existed.

- New public transport systems such as horse-drawn <u>omnibuses</u> and the underground railway allowed people to live far from where they worked, becoming the first commuters.

- The huge numbers of working families were housed in long streets of terraced, back-to-back houses. Often groups of houses shared facilities like toilets or fresh water.

- As people had little room for cooking or entertaining themselves at home, many new 'public houses' were built on street corners, providing food, fun and, of course, alcohol!

Urban poverty

In many ways, the Industrial Revolution and the growth of cities made the lives of ordinary people much better. Wages rose and there were more goods to buy. However, by 1900 men like Charles Booth and Seebohm Rowntree reported that about one third of people in cities were living in poverty, and there were few organisations to help them. This poverty affected people who could not work, particularly:

- the sick
- the disabled
- the old
- the very young.

One of the biggest problems was the bad housing. Victorian slums could be cramped, cold and unhealthy places to live, especially if three or more families were crammed together in one home.

KEY FACTS

↗ After 1835, cities and towns were given powers to rule themselves in new <u>municipalities</u>.

↗ Local authorities set up their own organisations to provide utilities like gas and water.

↘ In 1870, a law allowed local authorities to build elementary schools, which would provide basic primary education for everyone, free of charge.

↗ The mayors and leaders of the big cities also wanted to show how prosperous and important their communities had become. They built impressive new town halls, theatres, museums and many other places of entertainment for the benefit of their citizens.

EXAMINER'S TOP TIPS

Some important changes occur very slowly and would not have been noticed at the time.

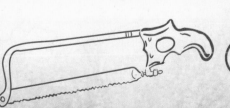

Hello? Hello?

Have you received something in the post this morning? When did you last make a phone call? What would life be like if you could only contact your friends by meeting them face to face? How do you get information about what is happening in places that you have never visited?

We are currently living through the Second Communications Revolution, but we must not forget how important the original Communications Revolution was in transforming politics, business and everyday lives. Even now, we are still benefiting from important inventions such as the postage stamp, the telephone, radio and photography.

It's in the post - The royal mail

A public post service existed in England from 1635, but the biggest improvements came in 1840 when Sir Rowland Hill introduced the idea of a stamp, paid for in advance, so that postage was the same wherever it was delivered. This 'Penny Black' stamp is the most famous in the world.

Dot dash - telegraph

This is one invention that no longer affects us directly, but it was the basis for much that followed. The first use of an electric current to send a message in code was in 1837, the year when Queen Victoria came to the throne. Telegraph lines quickly spread alongside the railway tracks so that messages could travel almost instantaneously across the country. Soon the network spread out across the Channel (1851), the Atlantic (1866) and around the world.

Changing times - newspapers

Early news sheets had existed since at least the 17th century. Newspapers as we know them today really took off in the late 18th century, however. When *The Times* was founded in 1785, there were already eight London papers being produced every day, but *The Times* is the oldest newspaper still published today.

The camera never lies – photography

Photography is another invention that seems to have many inventors. The Briton who contributed most to its success was William Henry Fox Talbot, of Lacock Abbey in Wiltshire. In 1841 he patented a system based on exposing specially prepared light-sensitive paper and creating 'negatives' that could then be made into prints.

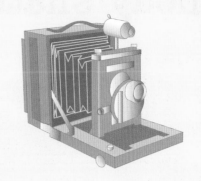

Hanging on the line – the telephone

Historians argue over exactly who should get the credit for the telephone, but most people still believe that the honour should go to Alexander Graham Bell, a Scot living in America. He was granted the <u>patent</u> in March 1876.

KEY FACTS

⬆ In the 1850s, the postal system was made easier to use by Anthony Trollope, better known as a popular author. He invented the pillar box, situated on every street corner.

➡ Telegrams were very popular in Victorian London and the Post Office employed hundreds of telegram messenger boys to deliver them and carry back replies.

⬇ Queen Victoria was very impressed by the telephone and she had several installed in her palaces.

⬆ The first use of photography in war was during the Crimean campaign in the 1850s. People safely back in Britain could see, for the first time, exactly what life was like for soldiers at the front.

⬅ In 1896, Lord Northcliffe founded the *Daily Mail*, which was sold for just a halfpenny and was the first 'popular' newspaper targeted at ordinary working people.

Body snatchers

In the early nineteenth century, surgeons and students of <u>anatomy</u> wanted to study how the human body works. However, the law prevented them from dissecting real bodies.

Some doctors in the famous Edinburgh Medical School were willing to buy <u>cadavers</u> that had been secretly dug up from cemeteries. This grave-robbing became a scandal and people were on the watch for 'resurrectionists', as the body thieves were called.

Burke and Hare found an easier way to make money. In 1828–29 they murdered 16 homeless people so that they could sell the bodies to their unwitting accomplice, Dr Knox. When they were caught, Burke was hanged, and his body was dissected by surgeons!

The scandal of Burke and Hare led to the government recognising that medical research needed access to real bodies to investigate. There were many other important medical developments during the nineteenth century.

Medical inventors

Edward Jenner is credited with developing the idea of vaccination against diseases. In the 1790s, he realised that deliberately infecting someone with cowpox could stop them from catching the deadly smallpox. It took some time to catch on, but eventually it was recognised that vaccination was a very effective way to stop the spread of many diseases.

In the mid-19th century, cholera was a much-feared disease that killed in the many thousands. For a long time most scientists believed it was caused by bad air, known as Miasma. In 1853, John Snow discovered in London that cholera was actually spread through contaminated water, but no one believed him. Outbreaks of cholera decreased in London almost by accident, because of the improved sewers and improvements in public sanitation.

Key medical inventions

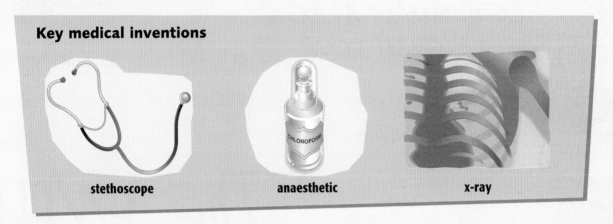

| stethoscope | anaesthetic | x-ray |

KEY FACTS

⬆ **The Public Health Act was passed in 1848, following a report by Edwin Chadwick that revealed just how high the death rate was for poor people in cities. A second Public Health Act was passed in 1875.**

➡ **Chadwick blamed the problem on diseases that spread quickly due to poor sewage systems, overcrowding in slums and the unhygienic conditions in which people lived and worked.**

⬇ **The law gave local authorities powers to improve public health by:**
- **improving sewers and street cleaning**
- **making landlords improve the properties they owned**
- **organising fresh water supplies for everyone.**

⬆ **However, in most cities little was done for many years because:**
- **costs were too high**
- **too few engineers and builders were employed by councils**
- **private landlords refused to spend money on their tenants.**

EXAMINER'S TOP TIPS

Every essay needs an introduction that explains what you are going to discuss in the rest of the essay.

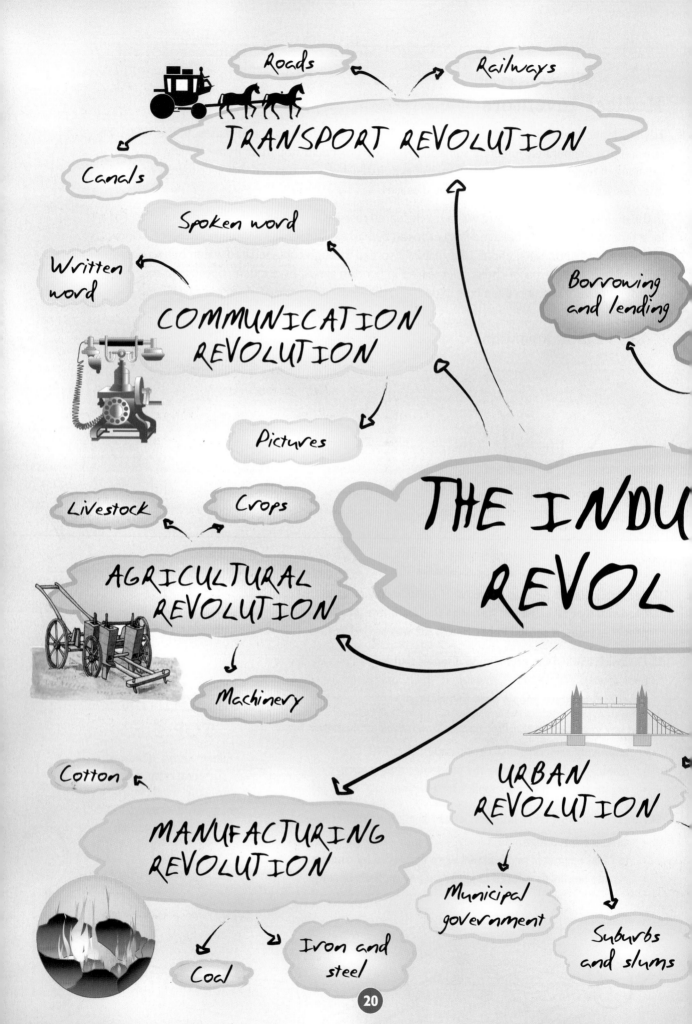

Roads

Railways

TRANSPORT REVOLUTION

Canals

Spoken word

Written word

COMMUNICATION REVOLUTION

Borrowing and lending

Pictures

THE INDU REVOL

Livestock

Crops

AGRICULTURAL REVOLUTION

Machinery

Cotton

MANUFACTURING REVOLUTION

URBAN REVOLUTION

Municipal government

Suburbs and slums

Coal

Iron and steel

Merchants and sailors

Imports and exports

COMMERCIAL REVOLUTION

The Great Exhibition opened in Hyde Park in 1851. Later, the Crystal Palace building was dismantled and re-erected at Sydenham in south London. The Exhibition had 13 000 exhibits and was a chance to display and demonstrate the many inventions and discoveries from around the world that had been made during Victoria's reign. It was also a celebration of all things British and was visited by more than 6 million Britons, rich and poor alike.

STRIAL UTION

Emigration and movement

POPULATION REVOLUTION

Rising birth rate

Falling death rate

MEDICAL / SCIENTIFIC REVOLUTION

Diagnosis of disease

Improved infrastructure

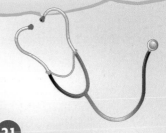

Cure of disease

Prevention of disease

Test your knowledge 1

1   Answer the following questions by naming the important historical figures.

a)   Who predicted that Britain's population would grow faster than the food available to feed them?

   ....

b)   Who invented the seed drill?

   ....

c)   Who introduced the Norfolk crop rotation system?

   ....

d)   Who invented the Spinning Mule?

   ....

e)   Who built The Rocket steam engine?

   ....

f)   Who built The Great Western Railway?

   ....

g)   Who promoted the ideas of free trade in his book, *The Wealth of Nations*?

   ....

h)   Who built the new sewers in London after the Great Stink?

   ....

i)   Who invented the pillar box for the Royal Mail?

   ....

j)   Who developed the idea of vaccination?

   ....

(10 marks)

2   Where did these key historical events take place?

a)   Where did the population rise from 17 000 in 1750 to 300 000 in 1851?

   ....

b)   Where was the centre of the British cotton industry?

   ....

c)   Where were the trials that The Rocket won?

   ....

d)   Where is the centre of Britain's financial sector?

   ....

e) Where did Fox Talbot invent negatives for use in photography?

....

f) Where did Burke and Hare carry out their murders?

....

g) Where did John Snow discover how cholera spreads?

....

h) Where was the Great Exhibition held?

....

i) Where was the first use of photography in war?

....

j) Where did production of cotton increase after 1783?

....

(10 marks)

3 Give the year to answer these questions.

a) When was the first population census in Britain?

....

b) When were the General Enclosure Acts passed?

....

c) When was the hot-blast system for making steel invented?

....

d) When was the Stockton and Darlington Railway built?

....

e) When were the Corn Laws introduced?

....

f) When were the Corn Laws repealed?

....

g) When was the Great Stink?

....

h) When were local authorities allowed to open their own elementary schools?

....

i) When was the postage stamp introduced?

....

j) When was the first Public Health Act?

....

(10 marks)
(Total 30 marks)

Let them eat cake!

In 1789, a revolution began in France that was to lead to the French king losing first his power, then his life. Eventually, it created a Republic based on the principles of Liberty, Equality and <u>Fraternity</u>, but it also caused thousands to lose their lives in the Reign of Terror, and it began a series of wars that would last for a quarter of a century.

Marie Antoinette was not interested in politics and did not understand the problems of ordinary people. When she was told that people in Paris were starving because they could not afford to buy bread, she is alleged to have replied, 'Then let them eat cake!' Some historians think that Marie Antoinette was not really as foolish as she has been portrayed.

Marie Antoinette, Queen of France

Louis XVI, King of France

The nobility

Worried that they might have to start paying taxes because the king was so short of money	Wanted the king to share power with them in the Estates General	Some were persuaded by the new ideas of greater equality in society

The professionals

Resented the fact that the nobles inherited so many rights and privileges	Influenced by new philosophical ideas about freedom and equality	Angry that the king's government seemed so ineffective

George Danton, revolutionary leader

Maximilien Robespierre, revolutionary leader

The workers

Suffered from food shortages due to very bad harvests	City workers had to pay most of the taxes, such as the <u>taille</u> and the <u>gabelle</u>	Rural workers wanted to be free of the restrictions imposed by their lords

Jean Paul Marat, revolutionary leader

1789

27 June 1789
The Estates General becomes the Constituent Assembly.

14 July 1789
A mob of Parisian <u>sans-culottes</u> attacks the King's Bastille fortress in the middle of Paris.

6 October 1789
A mob takes the Royal Family to the Tuileries Palace in central Paris where they could be more easily watched and controlled.

5 May 1789
Louis XVI is forced to summon the Estates General (the French version of Parliament). It is the first time it has met in almost 200 years.

> The Estates General was divided into:
>
> 1st Estate – the bishops and other churchmen
>
> 2nd Estate – the nobles
>
> 3rd Estate – everyone else (although this really meant the middle-class professional people).
>
> Although French kings preferred to do without it, Louis XVI needed the Estates General. The government's debts were so huge that new taxes were needed – and these had to be agreed by representatives of all three Estates. The king wanted the three Estates to meet separately, but when the deputies insisted, he had to agree to them meeting together as a single national Constituent Assembly.

4 August 1789
The nobles begin to give up all their feudal rights and taxes.

26 August 1789
The Assembly announces the Declaration of the Rights of Man

> The Declaration of the Rights of Man is based, to some extent, on the American Declaration of Independence. It begins with the statement that all men are born free and always remain free, and that everyone is equal in the rights that they have. These rights are listed as:
> - The right to freedom
> - The right for individuals to own property
> - The right to personal security
> - The right to resist oppression by the government
> - The right to be involved in making government decisions

EXAMINER'S TOP TIPS

The consequences of an event can often be divided into the immediate results and the longer-term effects.

Off with their heads!

1 When the French Republic seemed most at threat from enemies at home and abroad, a 12-man Committee of Public Safety was created, under the leadership of Maximilien Robespierre.

2 The Committee of Public Safety was given powers to do whatever was necessary to protect the young Republic, even if this meant abandoning the citizen's rights supposedly guaranteed by the Declaration of the Rights of Man.

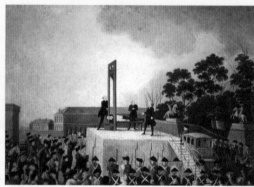

3 In practice this meant that the Committee ordered the executions of thousands of men, women and children who were suspected of opposing the Republic. The Law of Suspects allowed people to be accused for just being friends of other condemned men. So many people were sentenced to be executed that it was difficult for the authorities to keep up. They tried mass drowning and special firing squads.

4 A man called Doctor Guillotin invented a machine that could behead many people quickly and which could be transported easily from town to town. The guillotine is the ultimate symbol of the bloody Terror that overshadowed the ideals of 1789.

The fall of the French monarchy

1790	Louis appears to accept his new role as a constitutional monarch, sharing his power with the Assembly – but many people distrust him.
June 1791	Suspicions are proved correct when Louis tries to escape from France. The Royal Family are caught at Varennes and forced to return to Paris. For the next year, the king can barely leave his own palace.
April 1792	Revolutionaries such as Danton and Marat suspect Louis of plotting with foreign kings. They decide that, rather than waiting to be attacked, they should strike first. War is declared with Austria.
May 1792	War is declared with Prussia. Prussia invades France. Every man in France is told to get a weapon and join the huge armies needed to beat the invaders.
July 1792	The Duke of Brunswick, leader of the Austrian armies, issues a Manifesto warning the French not to injure Louis and his family.
August 1792	The King is accused of plotting with France's enemies. A Paris mob attacks the Tuileries Palace and the Royal Family are imprisoned.
September 1792	Louis is put on trial and found guilty of treason.
January 1793	Louis is guillotined, the monarchy is abolished and France is declared a Republic.
March 1793	There is a widespread rebellion in the Vendée region against military conscription. The rebellion is partly influenced by Royalists angry at the execution of the king.
June 1793	Disagreements about how to govern the new Republic lead to a fight between two factions, the moderate Brissotins and the radical Jacobins. Even in Paris, ordinary people are becoming critical of the authorities. Bread is now even more expensive than in the days before the Revolution.
October 1793	Marie Antoinette and her children are guillotined (Louis' eldest son died in prison).

EXAMINER'S TOP TIPS

Nothing in history is inevitable. Events are the result of a series of different decisions and the consequences of other events.

War and peace

Napoleon Bonaparte

1769   Born in Corsica
1785   Joins the French army

1795–97   **Military success in Europe**

> France invades modern-day Holland, Belgium, Switzerland and Italy, spreading its new political ideals. It retains control of these new republics, becoming unpopular with the people it has 'freed'.

Napoleon

1798   Leads the French invasion of Egypt
1799   Is made First Consul
1804   Makes himself Emperor

1805   **Battle of Trafalgar**

> Apart from a brief period, France was constantly at war with Britain. The British found it impossible to beat Napoleon, although they kept organising new coalitions against him, and they could defeat the French at sea and outside of Europe. Admiral Horatio Nelson was victorious against the French fleet off the cape of Trafalgar. But he was shot just as the day was won and died shortly afterwards aboard his flagship *HMS Victory*. Napoleon also defeated Austria in this year.

1806   Defeats Prussia
1808   Faces rebellion in Spain
1812   Invades Russia – the French are victorious but the army is then destroyed by the severe winter
1814   Is forced to <u>abdicate</u> and is exiled to the island of Elba. The French Royal Family is restored, as though the Revolution had never happened

1815   **Battle of Waterloo**

> Napoleon escaped from Elba and in 100 days he seemed to win back all his old power. The Duke of Wellington led an allied army of British, Dutch and Germans against him. Napoleon's forces spent all day trying in vain to break through the thin red line that Wellington had deployed on the ridge near the village at Waterloo. By the end of the day, as the Prussians marched in to join them, Wellington's army marched forward and the French army broke in two.

1821   Dies in exile on the remote island of St Helena

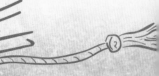

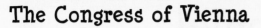

The Congress of Vienna

After Napoleon's defeat, the politicians and royalty of Europe had to decide how to bring order to a war-ravaged continent. A quarter-century of invasions across the continent meant that many of the old states had shrunk or simply disappeared, some had grown much bigger, and virtually every one of the old borders had changed.

The Congress of Vienna attempted to redraw the map. In particular, the number of separate states within Germany and Italy was reduced, although neither of these two nations were united. The peace was to be maintained by the great powers of Russia, Austria, Prussia and France. Britain was only partially involved in the new diplomatic system. Although this so-called 'concert of Europe' was not perfect, it is arguable that it established a peace that lasted for 100 years.

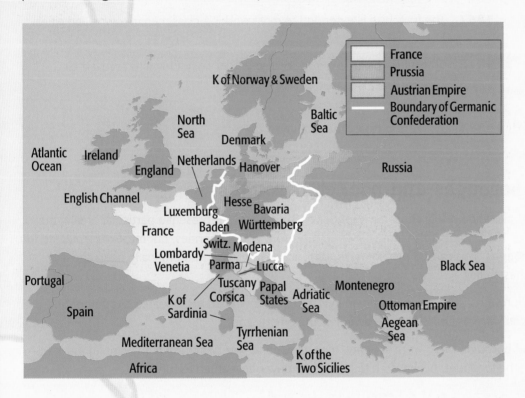

KEY FACTS

⬆ The Duke of Wellington was the leader of the allied armies that defeated Napoleon at the battle of Waterloo.

➡ Marshal Blucher was the leader of the German army that helped Wellington at Waterloo.

⬇ Horatio Nelson was admiral of the British fleet that won the battle of Trafalgar.

EXAMINER'S TOP TIPS

A good historian knows where the important countries are on the map, but this can be difficult as the names of countries have changed over time.

Power to the people!

1832 The Great Reform Act is passed; abolition of rotten boroughs; the <u>franchise</u> is given to middle-class men. However, despite reform, only 1 man in 6 has the vote, and the right to vote is based on wealth.

1838 The People's Charter demands more radical political changes.

1867 The franchise is extended to most working-class men in towns and cities.

1872 The Secret Ballot is introduced so voters do not have to reveal their choice.

1884 Workers in rural areas are given the vote.

Rotten boroughs and pocket boroughs

In Britain, we have traditionally chosen a Member of Parliament to represent a particular area in the country. Before 1832, some MPs were chosen to represent whole counties, but most were elected for individual <u>boroughs</u>. This caused problems, though, as the boroughs had originally been chosen several centuries earlier.

1 In rotten boroughs, such as Old Sarum in Wiltshire, the town had disappeared altogether but there was still an MP, chosen by the owner of the empty land!

2 In a pocket borough, there were very few men allowed to vote. As these men were 'in the pocket' of the local lord, he was free to choose whoever he wanted as the MP.

3 Some new cities, such as Manchester, had no MP at all.

The Great Reform Act of 1832

Radicals criticised the system for electing MPs. Apart from complaints about rotten and pocket boroughs, it seemed unfair that new cities such as Manchester were not represented at all. Middle-class men were angry at not having a say in governing the country. However, there were few radical MPs.

Tories believed the traditional system worked best, and they were worried that any change would lead to revolution (as it had in France in 1789). After 1831, the Tories lost their majority in the House of Commons, but they were still powerful in the House of Lords.

Whigs were wealthy aristocrats, like Tories, but they had middle-class supporters. Whigs believed that some limited change to the political system was justified to reflect the changes in society brought about by the Industrial Revolution. Like the Tories, they had been frightened by the French Revolution, but their solution was to make just enough change to satisfy the radical critics without going too far.

KEY FACTS

⬆ **The Reform Bill was passed by the House of Commons on three separate occasions in 1831–32, but each time it was blocked by the House of Lords. The Tories only gave way when the Whig Prime Minister, Lord Grey, made King William IV threaten to create enough new Whig lords to overrule the Tories. The Reform Act became law in June 1832, but it was still many years before Britain became a genuine democracy.**

The Chartists

Many ordinary people were disappointed that the 1832 Reform Act did not go further. In 1838 they drew up a People's Charter, or Great Charter, which had six demands, including that all men – but not women – should have the vote.

There were many meetings across the country in support of the Charter and a petition with a million signatures was sent to Parliament in 1839. This and two later petitions were rejected by MPs. The Chartist Movement lasted until the 1850s but it seemed to achieve little.

Despite some large public meetings and a few violent incidents, the Chartist movement was not very threatening. It was not well organised, the middle classes were frightened away by its radicalism, and ordinary people simply lost interest when the economy improved.

What the Dickens?

What does it mean to be human? What are we here for? How should we govern our society? How can we lead better lives?

These are very philosophical questions that men and women have been asking for centuries. However, between 1750 and 1900 four men named Charles set out their answers to these questions.

Charles Darwin

Arguably Darwin changed our view of what it means to be a human more than any other person. As with all scientific discovery, his theories built on the work of his predecessors, and they have been improved upon since his death.

In 1859 Darwin published *The Origin of Species*. In it he described the process of evolution, and explained how mankind had evolved from the apes. It was very controversial because it seemed to contradict what people had assumed was the story of Creation, as written in the Bible.

Darwin's work fitted into a wider scientific world that increasingly challenged traditional ideas about the workings of nature.

Charles Wesley

The brothers Charles and John Wesley were clergymen in the Church of England in the 18th century. They were critical of the Church's failure to teach the common people, especially in the new industrial cities. Charles wrote 6000 different hymns intended to be sung by ordinary people in the congregation rather than expert choirs. The Wesleys' hymns, and the way they preached to great crowds in the open air, helped to start a revival in Christian belief. They may also have channelled the people's discontent into peaceful religion and away from political revolution.

The Wesleys actually broke away from the Church of England to found the Methodist Church, but their example led to the Evangelical Revival and the Tractarian Movement. These groups had very different views about what the Church of England should be doing, but together they made the Church much more relevant in society.

While the Protestant Churches revived during the 19th century, the position of Roman Catholics improved, as they were permitted for the first time to vote, to become MPs and to go to university.

Sir Charles Trevelyan

Trevelyan is the best example of a Victorian official and administrator. He began his career working for the East India Company in India, where he promoted the idea of teaching Indians about Western science and philosophy. He finished his career in India too, after the Indian Mutiny of 1857, reorganising the police and tax systems.

The most important part of Trevelyan's work occurred in Britain. He helped to organise the relief effort for the Irish Potato Famine in 1846–47 and then he completely reformed the British Civil Service. He insisted on the principle that recruitment and promotion should be based entirely on merit, and his improvements meant that it became a professional, highly efficient organisation.

Charles Dickens

Dickens was a popular and successful Victorian novelist. Some of his characters are now amongst the most famous in English literature, for example Oliver Twist, David Copperfield and Ebenezer Scrooge. However, Dickens' work reveals a lot about social conditions in Victorian England – and this makes him useful for historians. In his own day, people found out about the poverty and deprivation around them through the fictional novels that they read. Dickens joined or inspired many popular campaigns aimed at improving society.

KEY FACTS

⬆ Charles Darwin made many of his discoveries on a journey to the Galapagos Islands on HMS Beagle.

➡ In 1851, only half the population actually went to church.

⬇ In 1871, the Army was reformed so that officer ranks such as Captain or Major could no longer be bought and sold and had to be earned instead.

⬆ Charles Dickens was a journalist and an editor of newspapers that campaigned for social change.

Up the workers!

Hours of work were long.

Britain prospered so the workers benefited too.

Health was affected by the living and working conditions.

Buying cheaper food and clothes meant wages seemed higher.

Housing was poor, often just slums.

Basic living and working conditions improved due to new laws and the unions.

Hard times

Better times

Was the Industrial Revolution good for urban workers?

The match-girl strike of July 1888

Basic living and working conditions improved due to new laws and the unions.

Annie Besant was a free thinker who supported a number of workers' demonstrations for better working conditions. In 1888, she helped to organise a strike of the female workforce at the Bryant and May match factory in the East End of London. The women complained of starvation wages, and of the disastrous effects of phosphorus fumes in the factory on their health. The strike eventually led to their bosses significantly improving the situation.

Trade Unions

Trade Unions are associations of workers in the same industry or factory. They were banned by the <u>Combination Acts</u> of 1799 and 1800 because the government feared they would organise a revolution. They were re-legalised in 1824.

For most of the 19th century, the unions were mainly for craftsmen and skilled workers. As well as putting pressure on bosses to get higher wages and better conditions, they were also keen to ensure that there was a big gap in pay between their members and the less skilled workers. Few women were allowed to join the unions at this time.

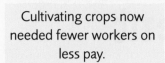

Cultivating crops now needed fewer workers on less pay.

Living conditions were often better than for city workers.

Common land for animals was lost due to the Enclosures.

Land-owning small farmers could be prosperous, at least until the slump in the 1870s.

Cotton mills meant that there was no spinning or weaving for country people to do at home.

Lifestyles and communities changed less and people could stick to traditional customs.

Country people suffered, because...

Life was not so bad, because...

Was the Industrial Revolution good for rural workers?

Rural discontent

Between 1811 and 1816, gangs of spinners and weavers, called **'Luddites'**, attacked the machines in the new cotton and wool mills. They were angry that they had to accept lower wages and were being made unemployed by the new technology. Their name came from their leader, 'General Lud', but he probably did not actually exist.

The **Swing Riots** occurred throughout England in 1830. Agricultural workers were angry at low wages and unemployment caused by new threshing machines. In hundreds of attacks, they burned barns and destroyed machines, leaving behind angry letters of complaint signed by 'Captain Swing'.

In 1834, six agricultural labourers in a town called Tolpuddle in Dorset were arrested. They had been organising a trade union and persuading new members to swear an oath promising to support each other. These **'Tolpuddle Martyrs'** were tried and sentenced to be transported to Australia for seven years. However, many people protested and after two years they were pardoned. Five of them eventually emigrated to Canada.

EXAMINER'S TOP TIPS

A source may be useful if it contains opinions and ideas, even if it does not have any facts.

Crime and punishment

At the beginning of the 19th century, execution by hanging was the sentence for around 200 different crimes. In London, public hangings at Tyburn attracted large crowds! Other crimes could result in a sentence of transportation, which meant being taken to Australia and made to work there in very harsh conditions. You could even be sent to special debtors' prisons if you could not pay back what you owed.

In 1823, the death penalty was abolished for more than half of these offences and after 1861 criminals could only be hanged for committing murder or treason.

Crimes punishable by hanging in 1800

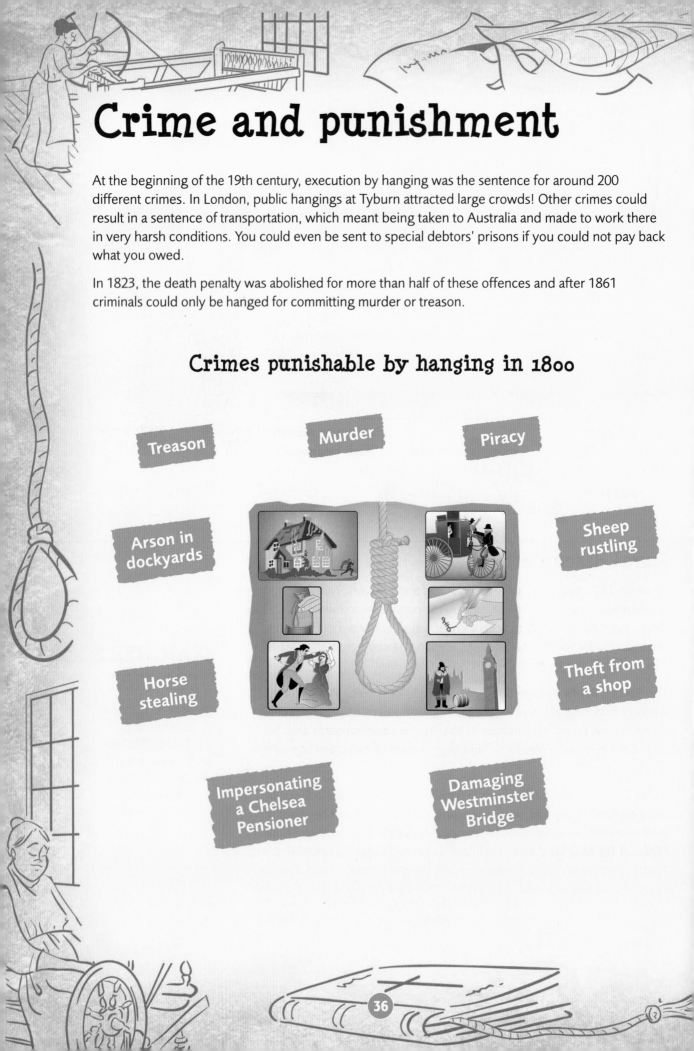

Treason

Murder

Piracy

Arson in dockyards

Sheep rustling

Horse stealing

Theft from a shop

Impersonating a Chelsea Pensioner

Damaging Westminster Bridge

Sir Robert Peel and the Bobbies

In the late 18th century, the only 'policemen' in England were local parish constables and a semi-private group known as the Bow Street Runners. The government relied on ordinary people offering information to the authorities, often encouraged by the promise of a reward. This was inefficient and could lead to innocent people being accused.

The Metropolitan Police Force was created by Home Secretary Robert Peel in 1829, and the policemen were nick-named 'Bobbies' or 'Peelers' after their founder. Although there were relatively few of these new police officers for such a great city, and they were only armed with a wooden truncheon, they were immediately very successful in reducing crime on the streets. Other areas of the country followed London's example, so that by 1860 every county had its own constabulary or police force.

Elizabeth Fry and prison reform

The most notorious prison in England in the 19th century was Newgate in London, but others were almost as bad for the dreadful conditions in which prisoners were made to live. Many prisons were just converted castles, and some were even the hulks of old warships.

When Elizabeth Fry visited Newgate Prison in 1813 she was shocked at the inadequate food, the lack of space in the cells and for taking exercise, and the poor sanitation. She began a campaign for reform that would last for 30 years of her life, and would continue after her death.

Apart from particular minor improvements in different prisons, the most important contribution of campaigners like Fry was to encourage the idea that even convicts should be treated humanely and that prisons should try to educate and reform their inmates as well as lock them away and punish them.

EXAMINER'S TOP TIPS

All essays should have a conclusion that says what you think is the most important point in your essay.

The weaker sex?

Angels: Florence Nightingale and Mary Seacole

Queen Victoria reigned from 1837 to 1901, longer than any other British monarch. She was not directly involved in the business of government, but she could be influential in many political decisions. She became the symbol of Britain and the British Empire, and there were immense celebrations for her Diamond Jubilee in 1897.

Despite her own importance, Queen Victoria thought that women were definitely the weaker sex – most of her subjects believed the same. Women from the aristocracy and the middle classes were expected to be respectable – this meant running the household and looking after the children (for her husband). Working-class women did go out to work, in shops, factories or as domestic servants, and at home they had many hard chores.

Nevertheless, there were advances in women's lives in Victorian Britain.

War is usually thought of as a man's world, but two Victorian women became famous for their part in the Crimean War (1854–56).

Florence Nightingale organised her own nursing hospital for British soldiers who had been injured fighting against the Russians. After the war, she championed improvements in hospitals and nursing generally. She was known to the British public as 'the Lady with Lamp' because of her reputation for looking after the patients even through the night.

Mary Seacole came from the Caribbean island of Jamaica. She wanted to join the nurses in the Crimea but she was turned away – the army officials were prejudiced because she was of mixed race. Seacole paid for her own journey and went all the way to the front line. Her 'British Hotel' provided the soldiers with food and supplies, and Seacole herself went onto the battlefield to help the wounded. She became very popular with the ordinary men.

Medical Lizzies: Elizabeth Blackwell and Elizabeth Garrett Anderson

Elizabeth Blackwell was not content to be a nurse. She trained as a doctor, but had to train in America as women were banned from British medical schools.

Elizabeth Garrett Anderson managed to persuade Middlesex Hospital to train her, before founding her own hospital. Eventually, in 1896, she helped to get the law passed which allowed women to train as doctors.

Literary Lizzies: Elizabeth Gaskell and Elizabeth Barrett Browning

In the mid-19th century, Elizabeth Gaskell was the most famous woman novelist in Britain. She is especially remembered today for writing about the changes brought about by the Industrial Revolution, especially the problems of the poor urban workers. Gaskell also wrote articles for Charles Dickens.

Elizabeth Barrett Browning was one of the most important poets of her day.

However, she was also keen to draw attention to political and social issues, such as slavery in America and the status of women in Britain.

KEY FACTS

⬆ Schools for girls. Until the Victorian era, it was assumed that girls should be educated in practical skills such as sewing and singing, drawing and dancing. Very few were taught history or mathematics or other academic subjects. However, private schools like Cheltenham Ladies College were soon founded, and from 1869 local councils could open girls' schools. At the universities, women could not take degrees but women's colleges were founded, including Queen's College in London and Newnham College in Cambridge.

➡ Votes for women. The MP and philosopher John Stuart Mill tried to amend the 1867 Reform Act to give the vote to women. He failed, and few politicians believed in female suffrage at that time, but the campaign to give women the vote had begun. By 1900, women with property were allowed to vote in local elections and to stand for election as councillors.

⬇ Rights for wives. In Victorian times, when women married, all their property and possessions were automatically transferred into the ownership of their husband. A new law in 1882 allowed women to keep their property for themselves even when they married. Divorce became possible for women after 1857, but in practice, the laws on divorce were still very biased towards husbands.

War with Europe

The Terror

REVOLUTIONARY FRANCE

The Rights of Man: Liberty, Equality, Fraternity

Causes of discontent

The Estates General and National Assembly

1789

Ending the monarchy and creating a Republic

POLITICAL REFORM

Napoleon and his enemies

THE NAPOLEONIC WARS

POLITICAL REFORM IN THE UK

The Great Reform Act 1832

Different political groups

The peace

The wars

The Chartists and the Great Charter

The English Parliament has existed since the 13th Century. It has two Houses, the House of Lords and the House of Commons. In 1707, the Act of Union closed the Scottish Parliament and Scottish MPs came to London instead. In 1801, Ireland's Parliament was also closed so that there was a single Parliament for the whole of the British Isles. The Palace of Westminster has been the permanent home of the English Parliament since the 16th Century. The old building burned down in 1834, and the Palace that we know today dates from this time. It was built in the 'Gothic' style that is so typical of the Victorian era by Sir Charles Barry and Augustus Pugin.

Government

Science

Religion

NEW IDEAS

Political and legal rights

Education and literature

VICTORIAN WOMEN

Victorian heroines

SOCIAL REFORM

Prisons

LAW AND ORDER

City workers

Country workers

HOW LIFE CHANGED FOR WORKERS

Police

Criminals

Trade unions

Test your knowledge 2

1 Answer the following questions by naming the important historical figures.

a) Who was the Queen of France when the French Revolution occurred?

....

b) Who led the Committee of Public Safety during the Terror?

....

c) Who defeated Napoleon at Waterloo?

....

d) Who was the victorious admiral at the Battle of Trafalgar?

....

e) Who wrote *The Origin of Species*?

....

f) Who founded the Methodist movement?

....

g) Who was the champion of the match-girls?

....

h) Who were transported to Australia in 1834?

....

i) Who founded the Metropolitan Police?

....

j) Who was the first woman trained as a doctor in Britain at Middlesex Hospital?

....

(Total 10 marks)

2 Give the year to answer these questions.

a) When was the storming of the Bastille? Try to include the day and the month as well.

....

b) When was the French king executed? Try to include the month as well.

....

c) When was the Battle of Trafalgar?

....

d) When did Napoleon make himself Emperor of France?

....

e) When was the Great Reform Act?

....

f) When was the Great Charter drawn up?

....

g) When was *The Origin of Species* published?

....

h) When was the match-girls' strike?

....

i) When were the Swing Riots?

....

j) When was the law passed that allowed married women to keep their own property?

....

(Total 10 marks)

3   Where did these key historical events take place?

a) Where was the French Royal Family imprisoned after October 1789?

....

b) Where was the French Royal Family caught when they tried to escape from France?

....

c) Where was Napoleon born?

....

d) Where did Napoleon invade in 1812?

....

e) Where was the Congress held which redrew the map of Europe after the Napoleonic Wars?

....

f) Where was the famous 'rotten borough' with no inhabitants before the Great Reform Act?

....

g) Where did Elizabeth Fry visit and criticise in 1813?

....

h) Where were Florence Nightingale and Mary Seacole nurses?

....

i) Where was Mary Seacole born?

....

j) Where did Elizabeth Blackwell train to be a doctor?

....

(10 marks)

(Total 30 marks)

Patriots or rebels?

The diary of King George III (so hands off)

Boston Tea Party

1773 Just my luck! American colonists, disguised as Native Americans, have boarded three merchant ships and thrown all the tea chests into Boston harbour. My government has retaliated by closing the harbour and replacing the town council.

First meeting of the Continental Congress

1774 Am I losing my mind? My American subjects have actually formed their own Congress! Have inspected some of Townshend's new breed of fat pigs – magnificent!

Battles of Bunker Hill and Long Island

1775 Those rebellious American colonists are still complaining about their tax bill and fighting my soldiers. And after all that we did to defend them from the French and the Indians! Sheer ingratitude ...

Battles of Princeton, Brandywine and Saratoga

1776 The colonists have now made a Declaration of Independence. They blame me personally for everything so they claim to be a Republic. How dare they? They must be taught a lesson in obedience ... And so should my lazy son, the Prince of Wales!

1777 America will drive me insane!

Battle of Yorktown

1778 My armies have now been beaten. Those meddling French and Spanish are sending help to the traitorous colonists, who actually call themselves Patriots. It is just not fair! At least I still have many Loyalists willing to stand by their king.

1779 Spain has declared war on Britain – bah!

1780 Holland has declared war on Britain – bah!!

1781 Disaster. General Cornwallis has surrendered at Yorktown. The world has turned upside down! ... Went for a walk in Kew Gardens to calm down.

Naval battle of The Saintes

1782 The Royal Navy has sunk another French fleet in the Caribbean. Hurrah for 'Jolly Jack Tar'.

Treaty of Paris signed

1783 Parliament won't pay for any more fighting and I have to make peace with the Americans. The Thirteen Colonies are all lost to me, alas ... I suppose I do get to keep Canada though.

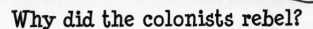

Why did the colonists rebel?

The people of the Thirteen Colonies in North America were Britons who had emigrated in the 17th and 18th centuries, often because they wanted more freedom than they had in Britain. They were still subjects of the British king, however; British soldiers protected them and they had to accept laws passed in Britain.

- American colonists had always been awkward, independent-minded people – that is why they emigrated originally – and they did not like being told what to do.

- After the French were forced out of Canada in 1763, the British colonists felt less threatened and therefore less reliant on protection from Britain.

- The British government thought that defending the colonies had been very expensive and they wanted the colonists to contribute towards the costs, but the Americans hated paying taxes, such as duties on tea.

- The British government ordered the colonies not to expand westwards as this would mean conquering Indian land, but the colonists thought it their God-given right and destiny to go West.

- Instead of compromising, the two sides both refused to make concessions on the basic principle of who should govern the colonies, so only conflict could break the deadlock.

George III

- King of England from 1760 to 1820
- took his political role seriously, but was unfairly blamed for his ministers' decisions, especially over how to fight the war with the American colonies
- appeared to become insane in 1788, but he actually suffered from porphyria Recovered until 1810, but had to accept his unpopular son as Regent from 1811
- always regretted losing the American colonies
- was interested in plants, animals and the agricultural revolution

George Washington

- was a prosperous farmer in Virginia
- fought as a British officer against the French in the Seven Years War
- was a leading member of the Congress and helped to make the Declaration of Independence on 4 July 1776
- led the American Continental Army skilfully, not just by defeating the British but by keeping his own army together and working diplomatically with his European allies
- was inaugurated as the first President of the USA in 1789

Aye, aye captains

… And so members of the jury, you have heard all the evidence about the <u>mutiny</u> aboard HMS Bounty in April 1789.

You have heard from Sir Joseph Banks, who told us that he had specifically recommended Captain Bligh for this expedition because of his previous experience of exploring with Captain Cook.

It has been explained to you that the expedition was instructed to go to the South Seas. The Bounty's important mission was to find 'Bread Fruit Trees' so that these could be re-planted in the Americas, where they would provide food for our African slaves that have been transported there.

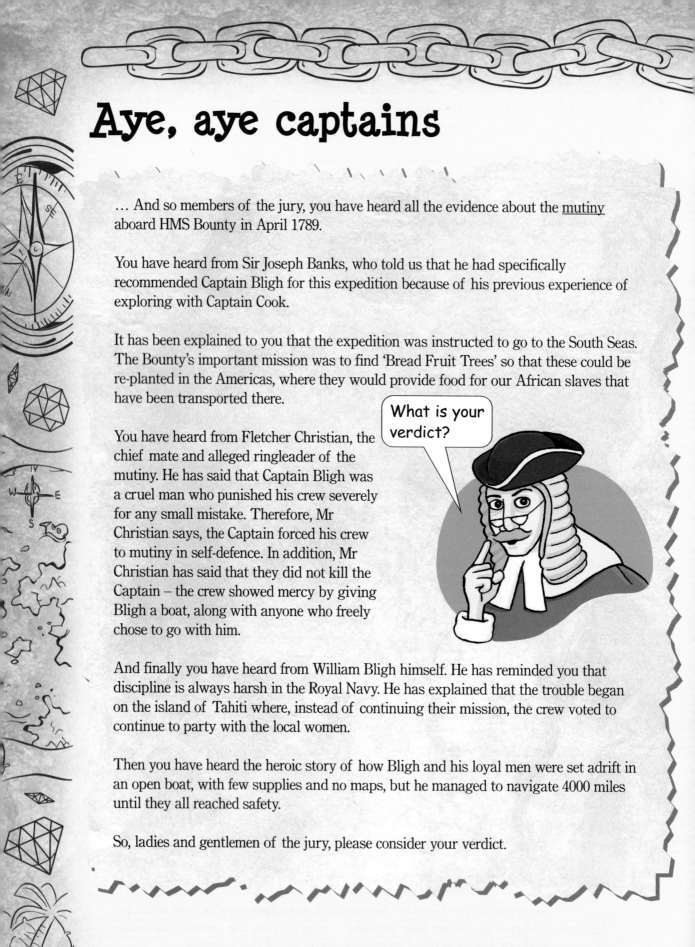

What is your verdict?

You have heard from Fletcher Christian, the chief mate and alleged ringleader of the mutiny. He has said that Captain Bligh was a cruel man who punished his crew severely for any small mistake. Therefore, Mr Christian says, the Captain forced his crew to mutiny in self-defence. In addition, Mr Christian has said that they did not kill the Captain – the crew showed mercy by giving Bligh a boat, along with anyone who freely chose to go with him.

And finally you have heard from William Bligh himself. He has reminded you that discipline is always harsh in the Royal Navy. He has explained that the trouble began on the island of Tahiti where, instead of continuing their mission, the crew voted to continue to party with the local women.

Then you have heard the heroic story of how Bligh and his loyal men were set adrift in an open boat, with few supplies and no maps, but he managed to navigate 4000 miles until they all reached safety.

So, ladies and gentlemen of the jury, please consider your verdict.

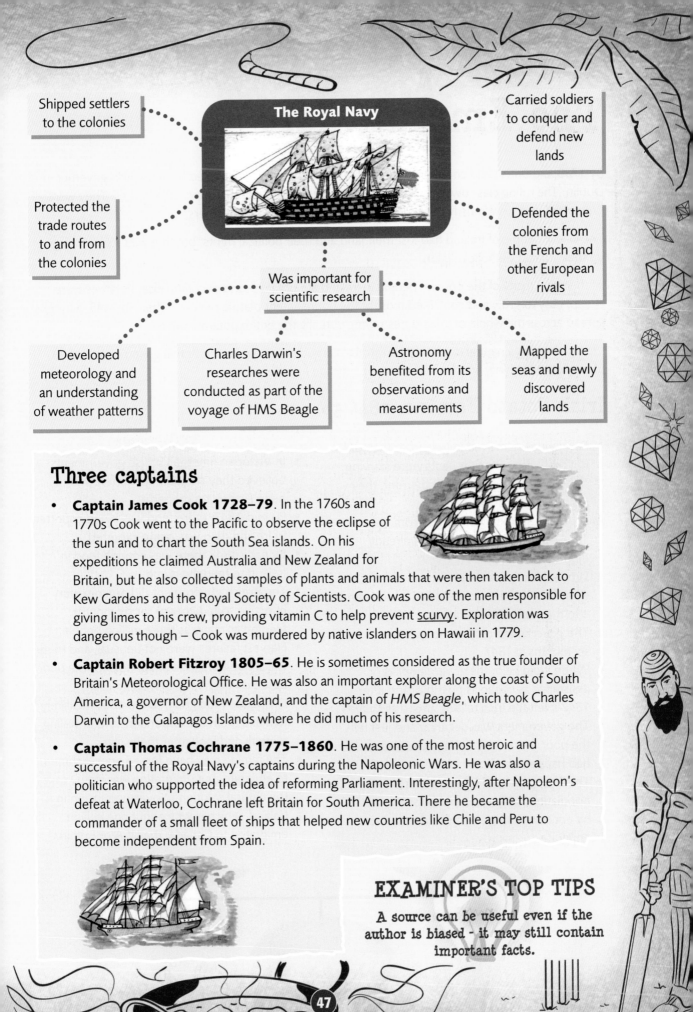

The Royal Navy

- Shipped settlers to the colonies
- Carried soldiers to conquer and defend new lands
- Protected the trade routes to and from the colonies
- Defended the colonies from the French and other European rivals

Was important for scientific research

- Developed meteorology and an understanding of weather patterns
- Charles Darwin's researches were conducted as part of the voyage of HMS Beagle
- Astronomy benefited from its observations and measurements
- Mapped the seas and newly discovered lands

Three captains

- **Captain James Cook 1728–79**. In the 1760s and 1770s Cook went to the Pacific to observe the eclipse of the sun and to chart the South Sea islands. On his expeditions he claimed Australia and New Zealand for Britain, but he also collected samples of plants and animals that were then taken back to Kew Gardens and the Royal Society of Scientists. Cook was one of the men responsible for giving limes to his crew, providing vitamin C to help prevent <u>scurvy</u>. Exploration was dangerous though – Cook was murdered by native islanders on Hawaii in 1779.

- **Captain Robert Fitzroy 1805–65**. He is sometimes considered as the true founder of Britain's Meteorological Office. He was also an important explorer along the coast of South America, a governor of New Zealand, and the captain of *HMS Beagle*, which took Charles Darwin to the Galapagos Islands where he did much of his research.

- **Captain Thomas Cochrane 1775–1860**. He was one of the most heroic and successful of the Royal Navy's captains during the Napoleonic Wars. He was also a politician who supported the idea of reforming Parliament. Interestingly, after Napoleon's defeat at Waterloo, Cochrane left Britain for South America. There he became the commander of a small fleet of ships that helped new countries like Chile and Peru to become independent from Spain.

The Emerald Isle

By 1750, the British had conquered the whole of Ireland, and it was ruled by an English governor in Dublin. The ruling class owned virtually all the land, for example the province of <u>Ulster</u>. They were all Protestant, and were mostly descended from English and Scottish settlers.

The Gaelic people of Ireland had lost their land and their political rights, but they had refused to give up their Roman Catholic religion.

At this time, many of the poorest people in Ireland ate potatoes and very little else. Potatoes were cheap, easy to grow and contained most of the nourishment people needed. Then, in 1845, a fungus spread across the whole of Ireland destroying virtually the entire potato crop.

Clearly this was a natural disaster, but historians argue over how far the British government was to blame for the famine, which killed about one million Irish people.

Irish Potato Famine, 1846-50

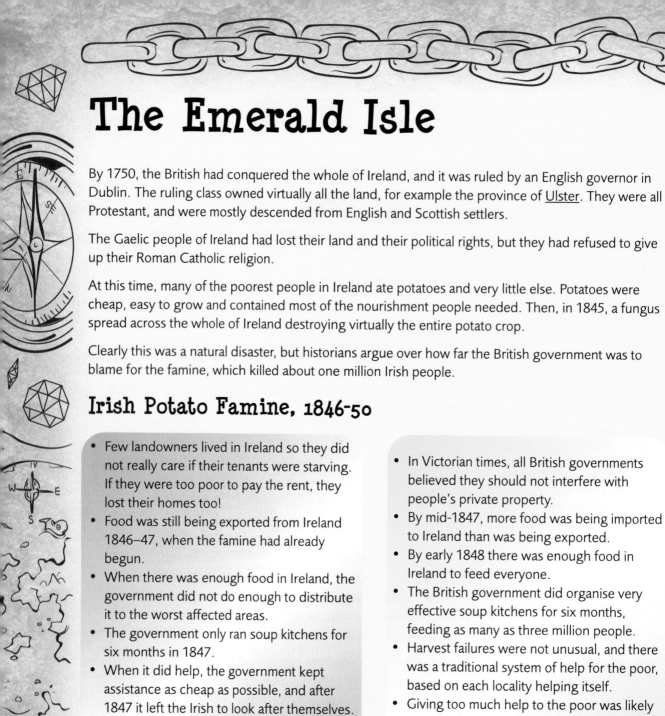

- Few landowners lived in Ireland so they did not really care if their tenants were starving. If they were too poor to pay the rent, they lost their homes too!
- Food was still being exported from Ireland 1846–47, when the famine had already begun.
- When there was enough food in Ireland, the government did not do enough to distribute it to the worst affected areas.
- The government only ran soup kitchens for six months in 1847.
- When it did help, the government kept assistance as cheap as possible, and after 1847 it left the Irish to look after themselves.
- The government was uncaring and just left the poor to starve as if they deserved what had happened to them.
- The British seemed to want the Irish population to shrink, either by starvation or by encouraging the poorest Irishmen to emigrate.

- In Victorian times, all British governments believed they should not interfere with people's private property.
- By mid-1847, more food was being imported to Ireland than was being exported.
- By early 1848 there was enough food in Ireland to feed everyone.
- The British government did organise very effective soup kitchens for six months, feeding as many as three million people.
- Harvest failures were not unusual, and there was a traditional system of help for the poor, based on each locality helping itself.
- Giving too much help to the poor was likely to make them too dependent and unwilling to work and look after themselves.
- The famine may have forced poor Irishmen to emigrate, but emigration was in any case the natural solution to over-population in Ireland, which is why about one million emigrated to Canada, the USA or Britain.

To blame   **Not to blame**

Tone and the 1798 Rising

Wolfe Tone was a Protestant lawyer from Dublin. Originally he just believed in giving full political rights to Catholics, but then he became more radical and demanded complete independence for Ireland. He was influenced by the French Revolution, especially its anti-monarchy republican ideals, and in 1791 he helped to organise the United Irish Society. In 1798, he led a rebellion, with French help, which was crushed at the battle of Vinegar Hill. Tone was arrested but committed suicide. After the rebellion had been defeated, the separate Irish Parliament was closed down and Irish Protestants were allowed to send MPs to Westminster instead.

O'Connell and Catholic Emancipation, 1829

Until 1829, the majority of people in Ireland were prevented from holding any office of responsibility, attending university or voting in elections simply because they were Roman Catholic.

In the 1820s, Daniel O'Connell organised the Catholic Association to campaign for Catholic <u>emancipation</u>. O'Connell was elected as an MP in 1828, even though he was banned for being a Catholic. Rather than face civil war, the Prime minister, the Duke of Wellington agreed to the Relief Act of 1829, which allowed Catholics throughout the British Isles the same rights as Protestants.

Parnell and Home Rule

Charles Stewart Parnell was an Irish Protestant MP who became the leader of the campaign to achieve Home Rule (the right for Ireland to govern itself while remaining a part of the United Kingdom). He managed to do a deal with the Liberals under Gladstone in the 1880s, but he never actually achieved his goal, and some of his radical supporters decided that only violence would bring independence for Ireland.

EXAMINER'S TOP TIPS

If a source was produced a long time after the event it describes then it may be more reliable and balanced because the author may have used the accounts of several different people.

The jewel in the crown

Interviewer: Miss Annie Besant, after your success with a few match-girls in London, you have turned your attention to the millions of people of India.

Annie Besant: I champion the down-trodden wherever I find them.

Interviewer: Indeed. But do the Indians actually deserve all this attention?

Besant: They are also subjects of Queen Victoria and should be treated fairly.

Interviewer: But how have they been treated unfairly? Are they not more prosperous and industrious than ever under British rule?

Besant: We have deliberately restricted their textile industries so that they cannot compete with our cotton goods from Lancashire. We tax them to pay for our government and our army. And all the major Indian businesses, such as tea growing and exporting, are British-owned. That's not fair!

Interviewer: Well have we not brought peace across the subcontinent, ending the destructive battles between the hundreds of war-like princes?

Besant: That is true, but we have created an enormous Indian army to use to protect the rest of our Empire, and we are still fighting the people in the Punjab and Afghanistan.

Interviewer: Well, we have brought law and order. We have got rid of bandits like the notorious Thuggees who used to murder travellers.

Besant: Again, that is true. We have also done our best for women by banning the old tradition of widows being forced to die at their husband's funeral. But we treat all Indians as second-class citizens in their own land.

Interviewer: Well what is your solution, Miss Besant?

Besant: We must allow the Indians to rule themselves but as part of the British Empire.

From East India Company to Raj

1600   The British East India Company, a trading company, is founded
1600s   The British open trading posts at Madras, Bombay and Calcutta
1757   Battle of Plassey; Bengal falls into British hands
1799   Wellington defeats Tipu Sultan (ruler of Mysore in south India)
1849   Punjab in northern India is conquered
1857   Indian Mutiny breaks out but is crushed the next year
1858   Government of India is taken over by a Viceroy for the British Crown
1876   Queen Victoria becomes Empress of India
1885   Indian National Congress is founded to campaign for self-government

Heroes and villains

In 1757, the East India Company, which was meant to be just a trading company, began the process of conquering the whole of India. However, a century later, in 1857, the British were almost swept out of the subcontinent by their own sepoy army. As a result, the British government took over the Company's Indian empire. This began the period known as the Raj. India became independent in 1947.

It is possible to write two completely different histories of the events of 1857...

The East India Company's Indian soldiers mutinied, turned on their British officers and then massacred whole communities, including 200 women and children at Cawnpore. The story of Miss Wheeler, who fought off mutinous sepoys in her bungalow, aroused anger in Britain. Even more notorious was the so-called Black Hole of Calcutta, where dozens of civilians died because they had been forced into a tiny prison in sweltering heat. It was necessary to send thousands of regular British soldiers to restore order.

The people of India were waiting for a chance to free themselves from the British and restore the Mughal Empire. The British made the mistake of insulting the religion of their sepoys because the Indian soldiers were expected to handle rifle cartridges smeared in grease from pigs and cows. It allowed Indian leaders like the Rani of Jhansi, who had had her lands confiscated, to begin a rebellion. The British army defeated the Indian freedom fighters in battle, but they massacred whole villages to punish them for the uprising.

EXAMINER'S TOP TIPS

Historians often disagree. You should be able to describe each view fairly.

Slave trade

The log of the slaveship Felix, recorded by Captain Theodore Lewis, in the year of our Lord 1772.

A fair wind has carried us out of Bristol with a full cargo of woollen cloth and iron tools.

We have reached the Guinea coast in good time. Two crewmen are suffering from sunstroke but otherwise all is well.

The cargo has been unloaded and sold. My employers will be pleased with the profits I have made, especially as I hope to buy even more slaves than we had planned, although we will be short of space.

I have taken on 520 Africans. We shall have difficulty coping with so many on the voyage, but it will be worth it providing not too many die by the time we get to the Americas.

We have lost another two slaves today. That makes a total of four adult males, five females and two children dead already.

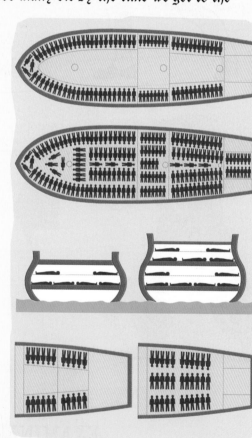

The stench from the hold is unbearable. If only it were not so hot! I confess it is partly my fault for taking more than 500 slaves onto a ship designed for no more than 350. Another three slaves died today, apparently from suffocation. I have also had to flog two Africans for disobedience.

Supplies of food and especially water are running low. The crew are on reduced rations. There may be little left for the slaves. I have doubled the guard in case their desperation causes them to rebel.

At last we are in sight of land. I have lost almost 50 slaves on the voyage, and I fear that another 50 or so will be unfit to be sold at auction. However, the rest should fetch a good price and I am very pleased that this has been such a profitable venture.

Who were the slaves?

- Most slaves were young men (likely to be the best workers), but women and children were taken too.

- They were taken mostly from peoples such as the Ibo and Hausa in West Africa.

- Later, the British and other Europeans established coastal forts and they captured local Africans themselves.

- When the slaves arrived in the Americas they were sold to plantation owners, often in big public auctions.

- Originally they were bought from other Africans and from Arab slave traders.

- The traders then transported the slaves to America and the Caribbean. In all, around 10 million Africans were transported to America as slaves, but as many as 2 million may have died on the journey.

What was slavery like?

- Slaves could be sold at any time, and their children belonged to their master, not the parents.

- Slaves almost always had to work for very long hours, mostly doing heavy manual jobs.

- They could be kept on a poor diet, badly clothed and made to live in very basic conditions.

- They might be beaten and mistreated (including sexual abuse).

- Slaves could not marry without permission from their master.

- Some plantation owners used iron collars and chains to stop them from running away.

- Any slave who did try to escape might be whipped or branded.

The triangular trade

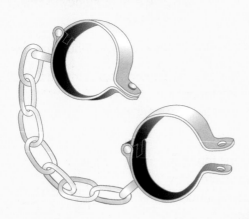

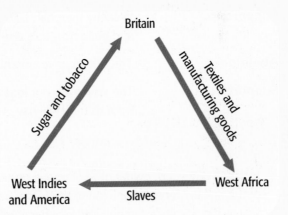

Britain

Sugar and tobacco

Textiles and manufacturing goods

West Indies and America

Slaves

West Africa

EXAMINER'S TOP TIPS

It is impossible to say exactly what life was like for slaves in the 18th century. What we can say is what slavery meant in legal terms and we can describe some of the things that happened to the slaves.

Am I not a man and a brother?

In 1787, The Society for the Abolition of the Slave Trade began a campaign against the use of slave labour in the British Empire. The following year the House of Commons debated the issue. In 1807, a new government finally got MPs to ban the slave trade in Britain. But it wasn't until 1833 that the trade was banned across the British Empire and all slaves were freed.

Abolitionist: The Bible says that all men are equal in the eyes of God, so how can one person own another?

Supporter of slavery: But the Bible often refers to slavery and it never actually condemns it. In fact it says that slaves should obey their master!

Abolitionist: Even so, stealing people from their homes in Africa is immoral.

Supporter: Most of the slaves are actually sold to us by other Africans.

Abolitionist: They are made to work on sugar plantations in appalling conditions.

Supporter: We tried using British servants, but Europeans cannot survive working in these hot climates, so we have to have Africans to do the work.

Abolitionist: But the workers don't have to be slaves, they could be free men who were paid for their labour.

Supporter: No one would do this work willingly. If we paid them and let them work fewer hours then the price of sugar and tobacco would be very high.

Abolitionist: The slave traders and plantation owners treat the slaves very cruelly and do not deserve to be called British.

Supporter: Wealthy merchants and plantation owners give a lot of money to charity and build hospitals and similar institutions in Britain.

Abolitionist: The British government simply should not allow such an inhumane system.

Supporter: The slaves are our legal property and if the government wants to take them from us they will have to pay compensation.

Josiah Wedgwood, owner of the famous pottery, was the founder of the Society for the Abolition of the Slave Trade. He created this seal as the Society's symbol. The seal became a fashion statement, appearing on plates, bracelets and hair pins.

Slave resistance

Individual slaves had little hope of resisting their oppression except by running away. In some parts of the Caribbean there were groups of runaways called Maroons who formed their own communities. However, there were some revolts by slaves:

1760 Jamaica   1763 Guyana   1795 Granada   1816 Barbados   1831 Jamaica

What about slaves in the rest of the world?

- Britain became the champion of slaves around the world. The Royal Navy was used to stop slave trading ships, and pressure was put on countries like Zanzibar to close down their slave markets.

- In 1861, Britain signed treaties with most European countries, all of whom agreed to abolish slavery.

- In the USA, President Abraham Lincoln abolished slavery in 1863, in the middle of the American Civil War.

- Brazil finally banned slavery in 1888.

KEY FACTS

- **Thomas Clarkson** collected evidence of cruelty inflicted on slaves in Britain and founded the Society for the Abolition of the Slave Trade.

- **Edward Colston** became very wealthy due to the slave trade. He used some of his fortune for the benefit of the people of Bristol, the city where he was born.

- **Olaudah Equiano** had been a slave in the Caribbean. He published his autobiography in 1787 and his story of the life of a slave shocked many people in Britain.

- **Sojourner Truth** was a black woman who had been a slave, until she was freed in 1823. She then campaigned against slavery in the USA.

- **William Wilberforce** was an MP who led the campaign to ban the slave trade throughout the British Empire.

- **Sam Sharpe** was a Jamaican slave who was also a Christian preacher. He organised peaceful protests against slavery.

EXAMINER'S TOP TIPS

A source may be less reliable if it is propaganda and the author intends to convince the reader to believe his own opinion.

Dr Livingstone, I presume?

Britain's interest in Africa developed relatively late. Although the British traded in African slaves during the 17th and 18th centuries, this only meant building temporary stations on the western coast. The first real addition to the Empire was at the southern tip of the continent, Cape Colony, in what is now South Africa, which was captured from the Dutch during the Napoleonic Wars. However, in the course of the 19th century the British Empire spread so rapidly that the Union Flag flew over a third of Africa, including the countries now known as Ghana, Nigeria, Botswana, Zimbabwe, Kenya and Uganda.

Robert Baden-Powell, soldier
In 1907, Baden-Powell organised a camp at Brownsea Island in Dorest for 20 boys, from both poor and wealthy backgrounds. In 1908 he wrote a book called 'Scouting for Boys', founding the Scout and Guide movement that today has 28 million members worldwide.

Cecil Rhodes, businessman and politician
Cecil Rhodes was a successful businessman and the chairman of the De Beers company, which controlled the whole diamond mining industry from 1888. He was also the Prime Minister of Cape Colony from 1890–95. In his will, Rhodes left money to pay for many students from the USA and the Commonwealth to attend British universities.

Dr David Livingstone, Christian missionary and explorer
Livingstone helped to spread Christianity in central Africa, and he campaigned to end the slave trade centred on Zanzibar.

On exploratory missions through Africa, Livingstone failed to contact the outside world for years at a time. The New York Herald sent the American journalist, Henry Morton Stanley, to find him. When Stanley located his man, at Ijiji in 1871, he greeted him by saying, 'Dr Livingstone, I presume?'

Zulu War, 1879 – military security

'First come the traders. Then come the <u>missionaries</u>. Finally come the red soldiers.' This quotation is from the <u>Zulu</u> king, Cetewayo, when asked why he would not allow a few peaceful missionaries to settle in his land. He had a point. In 1879 the British Government provoked a war with the Zulus and invaded.

Although they had few guns and were mainly armed with spears and shields, the Zulu army actually defeated the main British force at the battle of Isandhlwana. On the same day, a handful of British soldiers held off a Zulu attack on the mission station and trading post at Rorke's Drift.

Eventually, a second attempt led to the defeat of the Zulus and the conquest of their land. Cetewayo was captured and sent to Britain where he met Queen Victoria.

The Boer War 1899–1902 – military security

The British wanted to combine their lands in South Africa with the Boer Republics. But the Boers were determined to stay independent. In 1899 the Boers attacked first, hoping to win a quick victory and persuade the British to abandon their plans. In fact, the British reacted by sending a huge army to South Africa to conquer the Boers once and for all. They succeeded, but at a high price.

The British forces' initial aim was to relieve three towns being besieged by the Boers, including Mafeking, which was defended heroically by Robert Baden-Powell. It took an army of almost half a million men to defeat a Boer force of about 70 000, and the British even had to arrest whole families and lock them into 'concentration camps' before the Boers and their leader Paul Kruger accepted defeat.

Diamonds and gold – economics

Southern Africa did not seem a very important part of the Empire until diamonds were discovered there in 1866 and gold in 1886. Cecil Rhodes combined his business and political interests by turning the land of the Ndebele and Shona peoples into a new colony called Rhodesia (named after himself) – now called Zimbabwe. He also tried to get the British Empire to take over the independent Boer Republics of Transvaal and Free State, which is where the vast gold mines of the Rand were.

Christian Mission – religion

The European Christian Churches all launched missionary expeditions to convert Africans. From Britain, the London Missionary Society sent men such as David Livingstone and his wife Mary to spread the Gospel. In some places, the local people were hostile to the Christian explorers. However, the biggest threats to the missionaries were disease and the natural environment – Livingstone died of fever in Africa in 1873.

Give and take

There is very little left of the British Empire today, although Britain does still own pieces of land right the way round the world, from the Falkland Islands in the Atlantic to Gibraltar and part of Cyprus in the Mediterranean. Gurkha soldiers from Nepal still fight for the British Army, and Her Majesty the Queen is head of the Commonwealth of Nations, a club of 53 countries, most of whom had been part of the old Empire. However, the British Empire changed many things.

Culture

British culture has spread to the Empire:

- Many countries have English as their first or second official language.

- British political and legal systems have been kept in many Commonwealth countries.

- Cricket is played throughout the Commonwealth.

British culture has been changed by the Empire:

- Many words in the English language come from other parts of the Empire, e.g. bungalow, khaki, pyjama (all words from India).

- What we eat and drink in Britain has been affected by the Empire, from chutney to curries, from tea to gin and tonic.

- Polo, snooker and lacrosse all came to Britain from the Empire.

Emigration and immigration

People emigrated from Britain because:

- It was thought that there were too few resources in Britain to cope with a growing population.

- Communities of Britons would make it easier to control the new lands that Britain had conquered.

- Transporting <u>convicts</u> to the colonies was a useful form of punishment.

- Some people in Britain wanted a new life where they had more personal freedom than in Britain.

But native populations often suffered as a result:

- They might lose their land (e.g. the Maori of New Zealand).

- They might lose political power or freedom (e.g. the Zulus of South Africa).

- They might lose their wealth and economic freedom (e.g. Indians).

- They might be forced to adopt western culture (e.g. the Aborigines of Australia).

Pax Britannica

The British Empire helped to promote peace in the world because:

- The British became so powerful that most other countries avoided fighting Britain.

- Local people quickly discovered that the British were too powerful to resist, so they accepted British rule.

- Once they had conquered a territory, the British brought law and order, so there was less crime and banditry.

However:

- Other European countries were jealous of Britain's Empire, and there could still be wars over ownership of some colonies.

- Sometimes the local people rose up in rebellion; therefore the British had to fight minor wars all over their Empire throughout the 19th and the first half of the 20th centuries.

- British officials did not always treat white settlers and the local population equally.

Trade and prosperity

The British Empire created wealth because:

- It gave Britain access to raw materials and cheap food.

- It provided markets for British goods.

- The colonies benefited from new technology and modern industrial and agricultural methods.

- The colonies had guaranteed markets for their products.

- It brought so many different economies together that it began 'globalisation'.

- It promoted the ideas of free trade, not just within the Empire but everywhere.

However:

- The Empire cost Britain an immense amount of money to govern and defend.

- The local economy of some colonies could be distorted to benefit Britain rather than local people.

- Some people today are critical of globalisation and free trade.

EXAMINER'S TOP TIPS

You should explain several consequences of an event, but you should also decide which of these is the most important.

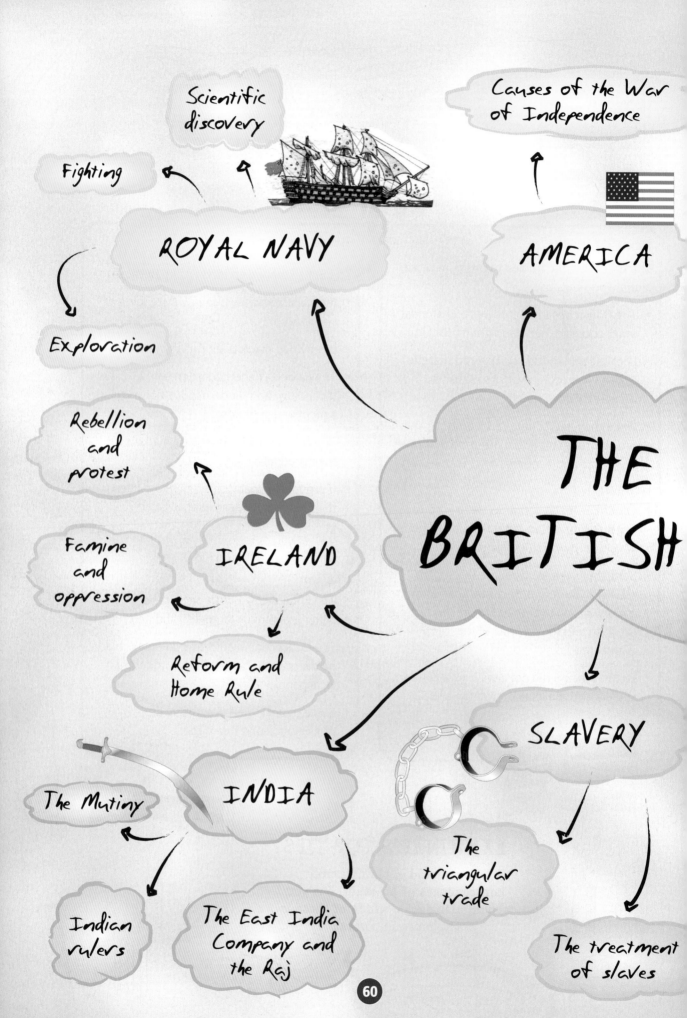

Scientific discovery

Fighting

ROYAL NAVY

Exploration

Causes of the War of Independence

AMERICA

Rebellion and protest

Famine and oppression

IRELAND

Reform and Home Rule

THE BRITISH

SLAVERY

The Mutiny

INDIA

Indian rulers

The East India Company and the Raj

The triangular trade

The treatment of slaves

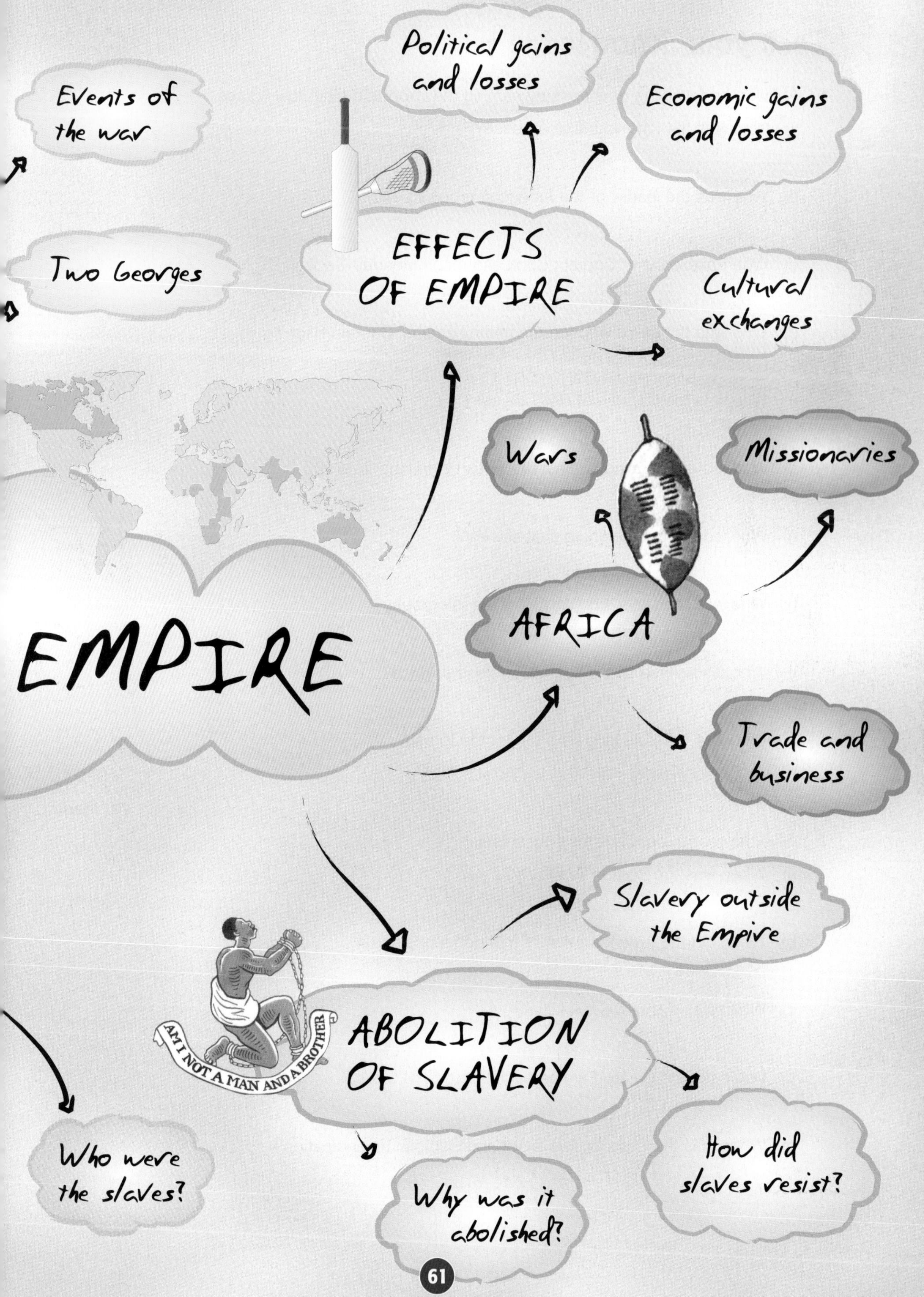

Events of
the war

Political gains
and losses

Economic gains
and losses

Two Georges

EFFECTS
OF EMPIRE

Cultural
exchanges

Wars

Missionaries

EMPIRE

AFRICA

Trade and
business

Slavery outside
the Empire

AM I NOT A MAN AND A BROTHER

ABOLITION
OF SLAVERY

Who were
the slaves?

Why was it
abolished?

How did
slaves resist?

Test your knowledge 3

1 Answer the following questions by naming the important historical figures.

a) Who was the king who lost America?

....

b) Who was the leader of the American rebels?

....

c) Who travelled with Captain Cook and recommended Captain Bligh?

....

d) Who was the sailor who led the mutiny against Captain Bligh?

....

e) Who was the Captain of *HMS Beagle*?

....

f) Who led the uprising against the British in Ireland in 1798?

....

g) Who led the campaign against slavery?

....

h) Who was the slave who wrote his autobiography?

....

i) Who discovered Dr Livingstone in central Africa?

....

j) Who was the Zulu king who fought the British?

....

(10 marks)

2 Give the year to answer these questions.

a) When was the Boston Tea Party?

....

b) When did the American War of Independence end?

....

c) When was Captain Cook killed?

....

d) When did the Potato Famine begin?

....

e) When was the Catholic Relief Act and Catholic Emancipation?

....

f) When was the Indian Mutiny?

....

g) When did Queen Victoria become Empress of India?

....

h) When was the slave trade banned in Britain?

....

i) When did the Boer War begin?

....

j) When was the Zulu War?

....

(10 marks)

3 Where did these key historical events take place?

a) Where was the Treaty signed to end the American War of Independence?

....

b) Where did *HMS Beagle* take Charles Darwin for his research?

....

c) Which countries did Captain Cochrane help to become independent from Spain?

....

d) Where was the Potato Famine?

....

e) Where did Tipu Sultan rule until he was defeated by Wellington?

....

f) Where was the so-called Black Hole?

....

g) Where did the Zulus defeat a British army?

....

h) Where was Cecil Rhodes prime minister in 1895?

....

i) Where was Robert Baden-Powell besieged by the Boers?

....

j) Where was slavery finally banned in 1888?

....

(10 marks)

(Total 30 marks)

Fair sex, fairer share

Two groups of women campaigned for the right to vote at the beginning of the 20th century. The <u>Suffragists</u> tried to use argument and gentle persuasion, relying on protest marches and writing letters. However, the <u>Suffragettes</u>, led by Mrs Emmeline Pankhurst, believed that more pressure needed to be put on the politicians.

Suffragette tactics included:

- Damaging public property, such as setting pillar boxes on fire

- Chaining themselves to railings outside 10 Downing Street

- Fighting with policemen

- Bombing politicians' houses

- Going on hunger strike in prison

The law was almost changed in 1910, but there was a <u>Dissolution of Parliament</u> before the Act allowing women to vote had passed through all its stages. In 1913, the Suffragette Emily Davison died when she jumped in front of the king's horse in the Derby race at Epsom. The Suffragette campaign was becoming quite violent by 1914, when the First World War broke out.

Some historians say that the Suffragettes had done enough by then to make the politicians give in. Others say that the Suffragettes only annoyed the men and that women got the vote in 1918 because of their contribution to the war effort.

VOTES FOR WOMEN

In 1908 a suffragette dropped leaflets over the House of Commons from an airship!

Political changes

1918	All women over 30 are given the vote
1919	Lady Nancy Astor becomes the first woman to be elected as an MP and sit in the House of Commons
1928	All women and men over 21 are given the vote
1979	Margaret Thatcher becomes the first female prime minister of the United Kingdom (women had already been prime ministers in India, Sri Lanka and Israel)

Professional changes

1900	Many women from poor backgrounds go out to work, e.g. in cotton mills or in private homes as domestic servants
1914–18	The government needs women to work during WW1. Thousands of women produce weapons in factories, and others work as clerks, drivers or farm labourers – all jobs previously thought of as 'men's work'
1919	Sex Disqualification Removal Act – allows women to take up professions such as the Law
1970	Equal Pay Act – men and women doing the same kind of jobs must be paid the same
1975	Sex Discrimination Act – bans any kind of preference for men rather than women in the workplace

Personal changes

1923	Rules on divorce are made the same for men and women
1945	Women are given a weekly 'Family Allowance' by the government for their first child
1967	Abortion is legalised in some circumstances
1969	Women are given an equal share in all family property with their husband

Feminism

During the 20th century, much was done to address gender inequality. However, some Feminists have said that this is still not enough. Since the 1960s, important Feminist writers have said that men will always end up being in charge of society unless changes are made to our whole culture, especially our attitude to families. If fathers are always the 'head' of the family, and husbands always get to make the most important decisions, then the rest of society will simply copy this pattern – a social system called 'patriarchy'.

EXAMINER'S TOP TIPS

When you are analysing changes in history, such as political, economic or social changes, you should look at each type of change separately.

Mud and blood

Life in the trenches during the First World War was unpleasant and dangerous. The fighting involved being bombarded, shot at by snipers, and gassed. In all, nearly one million men from the British Empire were killed, and survivors often suffered from shell shock and other forms of stress.

June 1916

Dear Ma,

Just a few lines to send you my love. There are rumours of a battle coming up, so by the time you read this we will probably have gone 'over the top'. I am rather nervous thinking about it since so few ever come back. At least we now have a chance to get our own back against the enemy snipers and artillery who have killed so many of my mates in the last few weeks. Anyway, I shall be pleased if it means we can escape from these awful trenches.

Conditions are appalling, I never knew I could get so filthy. We froze all winter, then we were awash with mud, and now we are baking in the sun. If I survive the battle then I may at last get to have a rest behind the lines. It will be a relief to get a decent hot meal and a change of uniform – at the moment I am scratching from all these lice, or chats as we call them. And then there are the rats that have grown fat eating the bodies of my comrades! Sorry for sounding so gloomy, but I am beginning to wonder what we are all doing here …

Your loving son,

Tommy Atkins

Was trench life that bad?

Conditions The muddy, exposed conditions were not so different to the jobs that most men had before the war, e.g. miners, farm labourers.

Cameraderie Unlike the French army, the British did not have a mutiny. Cameraderie was very strong within each unit, and morale in the army stayed high.

Commanders Generals have been criticised for being so distant from the frontline, but senior officers made frequent visits to the trenches and other officers lived with their men.

Casualties Casualty rates were similar to previous wars. More men died because so many more troops were involved in the fighting. The death-rate for officers was much higher than for private soldiers.

Comforts The men had many home comforts, especially when they got their regular break from the front line. Food was plentiful and nutritious, and often better than what men were used to from civilian life. Cigarettes were freely available.

Key events

4 August 1914   Britain declares war on Germany

6 September 1914   Battle of the Marne begins, ending Germany's Schlieffen Plan – the attempt to defeat France quickly in 1914 so that Germany would not fight France and Russia at the same time

22 April 1915   Germans use gas for the first time

25 April 1915   attack on Gallipoli in Turkey by forces from the British Empire

1 July 1916

Battle of the Somme begins

- The British commander, General Haig, wanted to break through the German trenches in a single attack by concentrating his forces on one part of the Western Front, by the River Somme.
- Haig also wanted to distract the Germans from their attack on the French at Verdun.
- He bombarded the German trenches with his artillery for a whole week, hoping to destroy the German defences, including the barbed wire.
- The attack began on 1 July 1916 but the battle went on until November.
- The Germans were ready for the attack and caused 60 000 casualties on the first day alone.
- In all, the British suffered 400 000 casualties during the battle, and only advanced about eight miles.
- The British used tanks for the first time, but there were too few and they were still too unreliable to make much difference.

31 July 1916   Battle of Jutland, the only major sea battle

16 September 1916   British use tanks for the first time

31 July 1917   Battle of Passchaendale begins, causing 250 000 British casualties

11 November 1918   Armistice ends the war

EXAMINER'S TOP TIPS

To understand the battles of the First World War, you should look at the 'big picture', what the officers knew and planned, as well as what actually happened to ordinary soldiers.

Listen with Auntie

It is impossible to understand the political history of our times without appreciating the role of the <u>media</u>.

1924
King George V makes the first royal broadcast

1927
BBC is given a Royal Charter

1929
First BBC TV transmissions

1936
King Edward VIII abdicated over the radio

1939
TV broadcasts suspended for the war

1946
Peak year for attending cinemas in Britain

1922
British Broadcasting Company (later 'Corporation') is founded

The BBC is nicknamed 'Auntie', like a friendly member of the family in the corner of the room. The name also implies that the BBC, like some relations, tends to think that it knows best what is good for us! The BBC's first Director General, Lord Reith, wanted 'to bring the best of everything to the greatest number of homes'. Reith's belief that the BBC was there to inform and educate people as much as to entertain them is still an important guiding principle.

1926
The BBC resists Winston Churchill

The BBC has always refused to allow the government to censor it. In 1926 it resisted Winston Churchill's attempts to use it to criticise the General Strike. Even today, many people around the world think of it as the most reliable source of news. In other countries, the media has been highly politicised.

1953 Coronation of Queen Elizabeth II is the first televised event to be seen around the world

1955 ITV's first broadcast

1964 BBC2's first broadcast

1967 BBC reorganises radio, founding Radio 1, Radio 2 etc.

1982 Channel 4's first broadcast

Using the media to promote governments

Radio

- In Nazi Germany, radio sets were sold cheaply so the people would listen to official <u>propaganda</u>.
- During the Depression in the 1930s, US President Roosevelt reassured people with his weekly 'fireside chats'.
- Radio programmes such as 'Workers' Playtime' helped to keep up morale in Britain during the Second World War.

Television

- Goebbels, Hitler's propaganda chief, was keen to use television to entertain people and persuade them that Nazi Germany was prosperous and modern.
- President Kennedy used television to put pressure on the Russians during the Cuban Missile Crisis.
- Party political broadcasts and advertisements on television have been used by politicians in democratic countries to win over the voters.

Film

- The German film industry expanded in the 1930s. Films like *Triumph of the Will* by Leni Riefenstahl made Hitler and the Nazis seem heroic.
- Lenin and Stalin used 'agit-prop' trains to take communist propaganda films to people in the countryside.
- During the Second World War, films like *Henry V* were used to encourage patriotism in Britain.

Using the media to criticise governments

Radio

- In the 1970s and 1980s, Western radio programmes carried news and music to people in communist eastern Europe which undermined respect for their governments.

TV

- The Vietnam War was the first conflict to be shown almost live on television and it shocked viewers around the world.

Film

- Charlie Chaplin's 1940 film, *The Great Dictator*, attacked Hitler by making fun of him.

EXAMINER'S TOP TIP

Use specific examples to help explain the point you are making.

Terrible tyrants

Name: Adolf Hitler
Year of birth: 1889
Year of death: 1945
Nationality: German (born Austria)
Ideology: Nazism (Fascism)
Title: Der Führer
Supporters: Brownshirts
Year came to power: 1933
Period in power: 12 years
Secret Police: Gestapo

Name: Benito Mussolini
Year of birth: 1883
Year of death: 1945
Nationality: Italian
Ideology: Fascism
Title: Il Duce
Supporters: Blackshirts
Year came to power: 1922
Period in power: 21 years
Secret Police: OVRA

Name: Josef Stalin
Year of birth: 1879
Year of death: 1953
Nationality: Russian
Ideology: Communism
Title: General Secretary
Supporters: Red Guards
Year came to power: 1928
Period in power: 27 years
Secret Police: NKVD

Name: Francisco Franco
Year of birth: 1892
Year of death: 1975
Nationality: Spanish
Ideology: Fascism
Title: El Caudillo
Supporters: Falange/Blueshirts
Year came to power: 1939
Period in power: 36 years
Secret Police: BPS

Communism: workers of the world unite!

Communism is the political view or ideology that believes in absolute equality between people of every race and background, especially in terms of their ownership of wealth and property. Following the predictions of Karl Marx, a writer from the nineteenth century, communists believe that history follows a clear pattern and that the last stage of history will see a revolution against capitalism by the ordinary workers. After this revolution, all businesses and farms will be owned jointly by the community as a whole and everyone will work together as a co-operative.

Real communist revolutions have not followed Marx's theoretical predictions. In Russia (1917) and in China (1949), the Communist Party – rather than ordinary workers – organised the revolution and the party kept control of government for itself. This meant that the leaders of the communists actually became more powerful than anyone else. Stalin was particularly tyrannical.

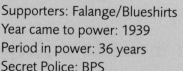

Fascism – believe, obey, fight!

Fascism is the political view or ideology that believes that inequality and competition between people is inevitable and good. The strongest and best people emerge from the competitive struggle as the leaders, who should be obeyed by everyone else in their nation.

All Fascists believe that the world is naturally divided into different nations, and it is inevitable that these nations will go to war. The strongest will make an empire out of those it defeats. The Nazi form of Fascism also believes in racial theory. They believe that races are biologically different to one another, and also that some races are naturally superior to others.

EXAMINER'S TOP TIPS

In order to understand why historical figures acted as they did, you should try to understand what their own political beliefs were, even if you would disagree with those views yourself.

KEY FACTS

1917 The Russian Revolution brings Lenin and the Communists to power

1922 Mussolini and the Fascists take power in Italy

1923 Mussolini removes all opposition to his rule

1924 Lenin dies, beginning a battle for power amongst other Russian communist leaders

1928 Stalin defeats his rivals to become leader of Russia, also known as the Soviet Union

1933 Hitler and the Nazis take power in Germany

1934 Hitler removes all opposition and becomes a dictator

1936 Franco begins the Spanish Civil War, helped by Hitler and Mussolini

1939 Franco wins the Civil War and becomes leader of Spain

1941 Hitler and the Nazis decide to begin the Holocaust, their plan to kill all Jews

Mr Churchill's war

We shall go on to the end. We shall fight in France, we shall fight on the seas and oceans, we shall fight with growing confidence and growing strength in the air, we shall defend our island, whatever the cost may be. We shall fight on the beaches, we shall fight on the landing grounds, we shall fight in the fields and in the streets, we shall fight in the hills; we shall never surrender.
4 June 1940, after the evacuation from Dunkirk

I have nothing to offer but blood, toil, tears and sweat ... You ask, what is our aim? I can answer in one word: Victory – victory at all costs, victory in spite of all terror; victory, however long and hard the road may be.
When he became PM

In war: resolution. In defeat: defiance. In victory: magnanimity. In peace: goodwill.
About Britain's attitude to the war once it was over

Winston Churchill

Give us the tools and we will finish the job.
To munitions workers

Never in the field of human conflict was so much owed by so many to so few.
About the RAF in the Battle of Britain

Before Alamein we never had a victory. After Alamein we never had a defeat.
About the turning point in the war in late 1942

The people of London with one voice would say to Hitler: you do your worst – and we will do our best.
About the Blitz

Let us therefore brace ourselves to our duties, and so bear ourselves that, if the British Empire and its Commonwealth last for a thousand years, men will still say: 'This was their finest hour'.
Rallying the people in 1940

On the home front:
- Conscription was introduced for men and women, for the armed forces and for important civilian jobs like coal mining.
- Civilians volunteered for the fire service and air-raid precaution service.
- Rationing was introduced for food, clothes and most goods.
- Children were evacuated from cities which would be bombed.
- The Blitz attacked London first, then other industrial cities like Coventry, then even cultural centres like Bath.

Around the world:
- The British fight in France in 1940
- In North Africa 1940–43
- In Burma and the Pacific 1942–45
- In Italy 1943–45
- In France in 1944
- In Germany in 1945

At sea:
- Merchant ships risked being sunk to bring food and supplies.
- The Royal Navy defended convoys in the Atlantic and Arctic.
- The Royal Navy fought German submarines and battleships like the Bismark.
- British ships in the Mediterranean supplied the army in North Africa and fought the Italian fleet.

In the air:
- The RAF supported the army wherever it was fighting.
- The fighters of the RAF defended the country in the Battle of Britain and the Blitz.
- The bombers of the RAF launched attacks on German cities and industry.
- The RAF supported D-Day, including taking paratroops.

KEY FACTS

⬆ September 1939	Britain declares war on Hitler's Germany after the German invasion of Poland
➡ May 1940	Germany invades and conquers most of western Europe; many politicians urge striking a deal with Hitler; Churchill is made PM and refuses to consider surrender
⬇ June 1940	Dunkirk evacuation; the Battle of Britain begins
⬆ Sep 1940	Bombing (or Blitz) of London and other British cities by the Luftwaffe; the RAF launches its own bombing raids against Hitler's Europe
⬆ Jun 1941	Hitler attacks the USSR
➡ Dec 1941	Japan attacks the USA; Hitler declares war on the USA
⬇ Feb 1942	Britain surrenders Singapore to the Japanese
⬆ Oct 1942	Battle of El Alamein; the British win the fight in North Africa
⬅ Jul 1943	Allied invasion of Italy leads to Mussolini's fall from power
➡ June 1944	D-Day invasion of Normandy; Russia fights against Germany in the east
⬇ May 1945	Surrender of Germany – VE Day
⬆ Aug 1945	Surrender of Japan – VJ Day

EXAMINER'S TOP TIPS

This section concentrates on Britain's contribution to the war, but you should also research the part played by the USA, USSR and British Empire countries in defeating Hitler.

Party games

For virtually the whole of the twentieth century, Britain had a 'two party system'. In other words, at each General Election, only two parties had a realistic chance of winning.

For the first 20 years, the contest was between the Conservative Party and the Liberal Party. For the rest of the century, the battle was between the Conservatives and the Labour Party.

The Conservatives have formed the government more often than anyone else, and a majority of prime ministers (PMs) were Conservative over the century.

Lloyd George

Attlee

Baldwin

Churchill

Blair

Macmillan

Thatcher

Liberal/Labour   **Conservative**

Today there are many different elections in British politics. The General Election is when the voters choose MPs to sit in Parliament at Westminster and, indirectly, they are helping to choose who will form the government.

Of course, different people will have their own ideas about which General Elections have had good results, depending on their political views. However, it is clear that some General Elections have proved to be more historically significant than others. This is often because they signified a 'turning point' in political history.

Turning point elections

1906

A long period of Conservative government ended and a long period of Liberal rule began.

The House of Lords lost its power to block government policies.

The Liberals introduced the old-age pension and other welfare benefits for the poor and disadvantaged.

1945

The first Labour government to have a clear majority of MPs. It won a 'landslide' (overwhelming electoral victory).

The government took ownership and control of many industries, such as coal mining and the railways.

The 'welfare state' was introduced, based around the NHS, an expanded school system and increased payments to pensioners and the unemployed.

1979

A long period of Conservative rule began after a decade or more when governments seemed weak and short-lived.

Unlike previous Conservative governments, Mrs Thatcher's was both radical in making changes and determined in being unwilling to compromise.

New laws were made restricting union power, government-owned companies were sold off, and the whole economy transformed.

EXAMINER'S TOP TIPS

Remember that sometimes people or organisations are known by different names or titles. For example, the Conservatives are also called the Tories.

KEY FACTS

Labour Party

- ⬆ Founded in 1900 by a merger of different left-wing, socialist groups, under the leadership of Keir Hardie

- ➡ Created by the Trade Unions so that they would have their own representatives in Parliament, and still largely financed by the unions even today

- ⬇ Traditionally believes in greater government control of the economy and protecting the rights and interests of working-class people

- ⬆ Believes in the Socialist principles of equality and social justice

Conservative Party

- ⬆ Emerged in the nineteenth century out of the old 'Tories', but the modern party owes its organisation particularly to Benjamin Disraeli in the 1870s

- ⬆ Traditionally believes in a government that was strong (especially on law and order and defence), but not too big (so it should not get too involved in running the economy)

- ⬆ Supports the rights of the middle class and people with property, so argues for keeping taxation low

- ⬆ Follows the pragmatic principle: 'If it ain't broke, don't fix it!'

A new Jerusalem?

The General Strike of 1926

What was The General Strike of 1926?

- The Trade Union Congress (TUC) called on three million workers in the key industries – such as railways, steel, building and printing – to leave their jobs and come out on strike.
- They also planned to get engineers and other workers to join the strike later, but they did not call on health or sanitation workers.
- The aim was to bring the whole country to a standstill and force the government to agree to their demands.

Why did it start?

- In March 1926, a government report said that ordinary miners must accept longer hours and lower wages in order to help reorganise the coal-mining industry.
- The TUC promised to stand up for the rights of the miners, but its negotiations with the government and employers broke down.
- The Labour Party and TUC leaders knew that a General Strike might look undemocratic, but the Conservative government would not compromise.

What happened?

- The government declared a state of emergency. It called out the army to protect food convoys and it employed 'special constables' to keep law and order, but there was little violence, apart from rioting in Glasgow.
- The authorities and their mainly middle-class supporters organised volunteers to keep the transport system and other <u>utilities</u> working. They even printed their own newspaper, *The British Gazette*.
- The TUC produced *The British Worker* to argue its case, and most working-class people supported the cause, but some worried that it seemed too revolutionary.

How did it end?

- The TUC agreed a compromise deal with Herbert Samuel, who wrote the original government report.
- The miners rejected the deal, which still involved accepting lower wages. The government refused to guarantee it would carry out the proposals that Samuel had made.
- By November 1926, the miners had mostly been forced to give in and go back to work, although some were sacked and they all had to accept lower wages and longer hours. The harsh treatment of the miners provoked bitterness that lasted for decades.

The Jarrow March, 1936

- After the Wall Street Crash in October 1929, trade between countries virtually stopped. The whole world economy suffered a severe Depression, and British unemployment reached three million.

- The government had to pay the 'dole' to unemployed men, but they tried to save money by cutting other spending, even paying less to soldiers and teachers.

- By the mid-1930s, things had improved in most of the country, but in some industrial areas they were still getting worse.

- In 1936, 200 shipyard workers from Jarrow, near Newcastle, began a march to London to protest about unemployment. Unemployment reached almost 80 per cent in Jarrow, and many people supported the marchers and signed their petition to the government.

The Welfare State

- During the Second World War, people of all backgrounds worked together to beat the Nazis. Many people decided that the spirit of co-operation must continue after the fighting so that there would be no return to the old social inequalities and there would never be another Depression.

- In 1945 the new Labour government promised a **'new Jerusalem'** by creating a welfare state that would look after people from 'the cradle to the grave'.

- They promised that the days of high unemployment would never return, and they also gave many more powers and rights to the unions. These union laws were only reversed again in the 1980s.

EXAMINER'S TOP TIPS

To make the most of this topic you should also read the chapter called 'Party games' as it looks at the different views of politicians towards the unions and workers.

All together now?

Even before the Second World War, some local people in different parts of the British Empire began to campaign for the right to rule themselves, or even to have full independence. Soldiers from all around the Empire came to Britain's aid in its darkest hour during the War, and it was clear that they deserved more recognition from the 'mother country'. It was also clear that Britain had been exhausted by the fight against Hitler and that it could not keep the whole Empire by force.

Ireland

Many people in Ireland had campaigned for Home Rule in the 19th century, and some even wanted complete independence. Irish Protestants, especially in Ulster, the northern province, were mostly keen to stay part of the United Kingdom.

By 1914, arguments between the two groups were becoming violent and each was preparing its own army. The First World War interrupted this conflict, but at Easter in 1916 the radical Irish republicans attempted a rebellion in Dublin. As soon as the First World War ended in November 1918, the Irish Republican Army began a new war against the British.

After a bloody fight, the two sides signed a treaty at the end of 1921. It was agreed under the prime ministership of Lloyd George that most of Ireland would be a separate country, within the British Empire. Most of Ulster was left as part of the United Kingdom, but with its own Parliament. Later, southern Ireland broke away to become an independent Republic called Eire.

In Northern Ireland, many Catholics felt that they were treated unfairly. In the 1960s they began to protest and violence broke out. The British government tried to restore order with soldiers and by abolishing the separate Parliament there. Meanwhile, the IRA began a terrorist bombing campaign, prompting the so-called 'Loyalists' to become terrorists too.

Despite several attempts to bring peace, this violence only ended with the Good Friday Agreement in 1998, and there is still no settlement of all the disagreements between the different communities.

Devolution

- Some people in Scotland and Wales began to argue for Home Rule in the 1920s, using the same arguments that had been made in Ireland.
- Later, the Scottish National Party and Plaid Cymru/Party of Wales were founded to win full independence from the United Kingdom, and in the 1960s they each won their first MP in elections for Parliament.
- In 1998, Parliament agreed to <u>Devolution</u> for Scotland and Wales, giving the Scottish Parliament and Welsh Assembly the power to govern while staying part of the UK.

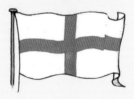

End of the Empire

1916 The Easter Rising in Dublin

1921 Treaty agreeing to the independence of southern Ireland, but within the British Empire

1931 Australia, New Zealand, South Africa, Canada and Ireland all become self-governing <u>dominions</u> within the British Empire

1947 **India and Pakistan become independent**

In India, independence campaigners had divided into two groups. Mahatma Gandhi and Nehru wanted to keep the whole country together, but Jinnah demanded the creation of Pakistan, a separate country for India's Muslims. When independence came, millions of Indians felt they had to move from one part of the subcontinent to the other, depending on their religion, and there was much bloodshed.

1948 Southern Ireland, or Eire, becomes a Republic

1957 **Ghana becomes independent**

Britain had tried to hang onto the rest of its colonies, especially in Africa. However, Ghana was made independent in 1957 as was Malaysia, and within 20 years most of the other colonies and territories had left the Empire and become voluntary members of the <u>Commonwealth</u> instead.

1967 The Catholic Civil Rights movement and the 'Troubles' begin in Northern Ireland

1972 The separate, devolved Northern Ireland Parliament is abolished

1973 **The UK joins the Common Market or European Economic Community**

The European Union, previously known as the EEC or Common Market, was created in 1957. Originally Britain did not want to become a member, and when it changed its mind in the 1960s the French refused to agree to let Britain in. The nature of the European Union has changed a lot since then, especially after the Maastricht Treaty of 1992, and the EU rules and regulations have become more important in deciding what happens in Britain. This has meant that membership of the EU has become a very controversial issue in British politics.

1992 The Maastricht Treaty agrees to the idea of 'ever closer union' between the member countries of the European Union

1998 Devolution is granted to Scotland and Wales, and the Good Friday Agreement is made in Ireland

EXAMINER'S TOP TIPS

In essays, you don't need to put down every fact that you know, but you should always have at least one example to illustrate or support the point you have made.

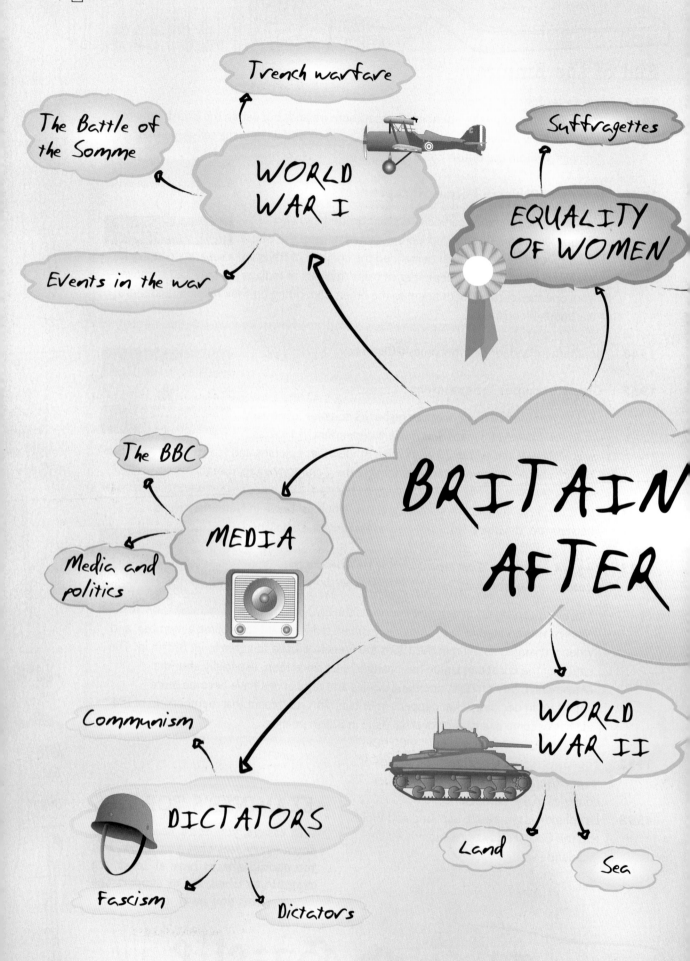

Trench warfare

The Battle of
the Somme

WORLD
WAR I

Suffragettes

EQUALITY
OF WOMEN

Events in the war

The BBC

MEDIA

Media and
politics

BRITAIN
AFTER

Communism

DICTATORS

Fascism

Dictators

WORLD
WAR II

Land

Sea

European Union

End of empire

UNITED
KINGDOM

Ireland

Women in the
workplace

General
Strike 1926

WORKERS
AND
UNIONS

Jarrow
March
1936

1900

Welfare
State

Air

POLITICS

Labour party

Conservative
party

General
Elections

Test your knowledge 4

1   Answer the following questions by naming the important historical figures.

a)   Who was the first Director General of the BBC?

....

b)   Who was the dictator in Italy in the 1920s and 1930s?

....

c)   Who took power in Spain after the Civil War?

....

d)   Who was the leader of the Suffragettes?

....

e)   Who won the General Election of 1979?

....

f)   Who was British Prime minister for most of the Second World War?

....

g)   Who was the British commander at the Battle of the Somme?

....

h)   Who was the first British monarch to give a radio broadcast?

....

i)   Who was the first woman MP to sit in Parliament at Westminster?

....

j)   Who was the Prime minister who agreed to the independence of southern Ireland?

....

(10 marks)

2   Give the year to answer these questions.

a)   When was the BBC founded?

....

b)   When did the Spanish Civil War begin?

....

c)   When did Hitler take power in Germany?

....

d)   When was the General Strike?

....

e)   When was the Jarrow March?

....

f) When were women over 30 given the vote?

....

g) When was the Battle of the Somme?

....

h) When was the Easter Rising in Ireland?

....

i) When was the evacuation of British soldiers from France in World War II?

....

j) When was D-Day during World War II?

....

(10 marks)

3 Where did these key historical events take place?

a) Where did the Jarrow marchers go to?

....

b) Where was Stalin the dictator in the 1930s and 1940s?

....

c) Where was the only violence during the General Strike?

....

d) Where in Ireland was the Easter Rising?

....

e) Where were the beaches from which British troops were evacuated in World War II?

....

f) Where did a Suffragette die when she ran in front of the king's horse?

....

g) Where did the British win a major victory in North Africa during World War II?

....

h) Where does the British Parliament meet?

....

i) Where did forces from the British Empire attack on 25 April 1915?

....

j) Where did Lenin start a Revolution in 1917?

....

(10 marks)

(Total 30 marks)

Practice paper 1

There are two types of essay question in this section.

The Section A essays are narrative: they ask you to describe an event – to tell its story.

1 You should begin the essay by saying what you are going to write about, including basic details such as the dates.

2 You should find **three** different features or aspects of the event to describe, or perhaps **three** separate stages of the story you are telling.

3 Each of these aspects/stages should be covered in a **separate** paragraph.

4 Don't forget to include lots of facts (dates, names and places) wherever possible and relevant.

The Section B essays are analytical: they ask you to identify and analyse the causes and consequences of historical events.

1 You should begin your essay by saying clearly what event you are going to explain, including some basic background details and what the **most important** cause or consequence was, in your opinion.

2 You should then write about at least **two** different reasons **why** that cause/consequence was so significant.

3 If you can, mention **another** cause/consequence that was important, but show why it was not as important as the one you have concentrated on.

All of the questions on this page deal with the Industrial Revolution. Each essay is worth 10 marks.

Section A Narrative essays

1   What happened to Britain's population between 1750 and 1900?

2   Describe the Agricultural Revolution in Britain in the 18th century.

3   Describe the changes in British industry in the 18th century.

4   What changed for British travellers during the Transport Revolution?

5   How did Britain's trade increase in the 18th and 19th centuries?

6   What happened to Britain's cities in the 18th and 19th centuries?

7   How did communications improve in Britain between 1750 and 1900?

8   How was the health of the British people improved during the 18th and 19th centuries?

Section B Analytical essays

1   Why did Britain's population increase by so much between 1750 and 1900?

2   What was the most important consequence of the increase in population in Britain between 1750 and 1900?

3   What was the most important aspect of the Agricultural Revolution of the 18th century?

4   Which aspect of the Industrial Revolution had the most important consequences for people in Britain?

5   Why was the invention of the railways so important for Britain?

6   What was the most important reason for the expansion of British trade in the 18th and 19th centuries?

7   What was the most important reason for the improvements in health between 1750 and 1900?

8   Which was the most important improvement in communications during the 18th and 19th centuries?

REMEMBER: To give a full answer to these questions you should do some additional research.

Practice paper 2

There are two types of essay question in this section.

The first type (Section A and Section B) asks you to either:

Describe someone important, or an institution or group of people (Section A)

or:

Tell the history of a particular part of the world during the period 1750–1900 (Section B)

1   You should begin the essay by saying which historical character/organisation or part of the world you are going to describe, giving their basic details.

2   You should find **three** different aspects of their career to discuss, or **three** important developments in that country during the period.

3   Include any important events in which they were involved.

4   Don't forget to include all the relevant facts (names of other important people at that time, dates of events, places visited, etc).

The second type (Section C and Section D) asks you to either:

Explain what made a particular historical character so important or what their greatest success was (section C)

or:

Explain why a region or country was so important (section D)

1   You should begin by saying what you are going to explain.

2   Then you should find at least **two** reasons **why** they were a success or so important.

3   You could mention other important people, or other successes they had, or other important places in order to compare them.

All of the questions on this page deal with the British Empire. Each essay is worth 10 marks.

Section A Descriptive essays

1 Describe the career of an important officer in the Royal Navy in the period 1750 to 1900.

2 Describe the career of an important British soldier in the period 1750 to 1900.

3 Describe the career of an important British woman in the period 1750 to 1900.

4 Describe the career of an important Irish politician in the period 1750 to 1900.

Section B Descriptive essays

1 What changes were there in Lancashire and the north-west of England between 1750 and 1900?

2 How did London change between 1750 and 1900?

3 Describe Britain's involvement in India between 1750 and 1900.

4 Describe events in America in the 18th century.

Section C Assessment or explanation essays

1 Who made the most important contribution to scientific knowledge in the 19th century?

2 What was the Royal Navy's most important contribution to the British Empire between 1750 and 1900?

3 What was the most significant change in the role and status of women in Britain between 1750 and 1900?

4 What was the most significant improvement in the life of ordinary working people in Britain between 1750 and 1900?

Section D Assessment or explanation essays

1 Why was the Potato Famine so devastating in its impact on Ireland?

2 Why were Europeans so interested in Africa between 1750 and 1900?

3 What was the most important contribution of India to the British Empire between 1750 and 1900?

4 What was the most important contribution of the Empire to the development of Britain between 1750 and 1900?

> REMEMBER: The different stories and sections in this book are all linked. For example, there are references to the Royal Navy in several different chapters.
>
> In addition, you could do your own research into any of the events or people that have interested you. That would give you more information to include in your essay.

Practice paper 3

Study the six sources on these two pages. Use the sources and the introductory passage to answer the questions.

On 22 June 1897, her subjects celebrated the 60th anniversary of Queen Victoria's accession. The Queen, joined by 11 Prime ministers from countries in the Empire, attended a service in the open air outside St Paul's Cathedral. A parade of 50 000 soldiers from across the world marched through the streets of London. On 26 June the Queen reviewed a massive fleet of Royal Navy ships at Spithead. In communities throughout Britain and from Canada to Australia, India to South Africa, ordinary people joined in the celebrations. Not everyone was impressed, however, and republicans criticised the whole event.

A

Queen Victoria at the Diamond Jubilee

B

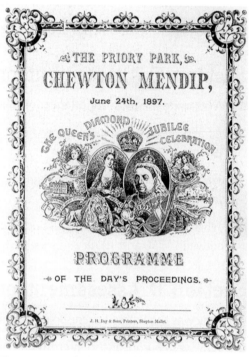

Front cover of the programme for the Chewton Mendip celebration

C

'Our little village was quite festive last Tuesday, when Brockham celebrated what is commonly known as Jubilee day. The houses round the green and elsewhere were made quite pretty with bunting and flags of all descriptions, and everyone did their best to prove their loyalty and show their sympathy with the undertaking.'

From the Parish newsletter of the village of Brockham, June 1897.

D

'...the Irish Socialist Republican Party, which from its beginnings has never hesitated to proclaim its unswerving hostility to the British Crown ... takes this opportunity of hurling at the heads of all who grovel at the shrine of royalty the contempt and hatred of the Irish revolutionary democracy. We at least are not loyal men; we confess to having more respect and honour for the scruffiest child of the poorest labourer in Ireland today than for any descendant of the long list of murderers and madmen who have sat upon the throne of England.'

From a leaflet issued in 1897 by Irish republicans.

E

The Review at Spithead.

F

SPITHEAD. JUNE 26.

A cartoon in the magazine *Punch*.

1 What can we learn from source A about the celebrations for the Diamond Jubilee?

2 What can we learn from source B about attitudes towards the Diamond Jubilee?

3 Look at source D. How does this source disagree with the evidence of sources B and C?

4 Look at sources E and F. Which source is more reliable as a record of the Review of the Navy at Spithead in 1897?

5 'The Diamond Jubilee was popular with all Queen Victoria's subjects.' Using all the sources and your own knowledge, say how far you agree with this statement.

Glossary

Abdicate When a king or emperor voluntarily gives up their throne.

Anatomy The study of the bodies of living things.

Borough A town or a district in a large city.

Brissotins One of the groups formed by the less extreme politicians in France, after the Revolution.

Cadaver A dead body.

Camaraderie The friendship that is created between people sharing difficult experiences.

Census An investigation of how many people live in a country, sometimes including other details, such as their age.

Colony Land that is part of an Empire and often contains communities that have settled there from the mother-country.

Combination Acts Laws forbidding workers to form unions.

Commonwealth The modern-day association of countries previously in the British Empire.

Congregation The community that meets in a church.

Conscription A law allowing the government to force people to join the army.

Convict Someone found guilty of a crime and imprisoned.

Convoy When transport ships are grouped together to make it easier to protect them.

Crop rotation When different crops are grown in a field, one after the other.

Democracy When the government is chosen in an election and everyone in society has a vote.

Depression The collapse of the economies of capitalist countries in the 1930s.

Devolution When the central or national government gives away some of its power to a local or regional government.

Dole A weekly payment to unemployed workers.

Dissolution of Parliament When a Parliament is closed and an election is called to choose new MPs.

Dominion A former British colony that had been granted the right of self-government.

Emancipation A legal change giving people freedom.

Emigration People leaving a country to live abroad.

Enclosure Dividing very large open fields between different farms, using fences or hedges around the smaller fields.

Fallow When a field is left without any crops.

Feminism The political belief that women are discriminated against in society.

Fenland An area of marshes and low-lying pastures.

Franchise The right to vote.

Fraternity Brotherhood, or treating everyone with respect.

Gabelle A French word for the tax on salt before the Revolution. It made buying salt very expensive.

Jacobins The most extreme group of politicians in France after the Revolution, particularly during the Terror.

Jubilee Celebration for the anniversary of a king or queen coming to the throne.

Media The sources of news and information, typically newspapers or television.

Missionary Someone who tries to persuade others to believe in their religion.

Mughal Empire The Muslim Empire in northern India which the British broke up.

Municipality A town or city council.

Mutiny A rebellion by soldiers or sailors.

Omnibus The original word for a bus.

Patent A legal right to be known as the inventor of something so that only the person owning the patent can profit from the invention.

Plantation A very large farm for growing crops such as sugar or rubber-trees.

Prime minister The most powerful politician in a country, who leads the government and has the final say on government decisions.

Propaganda The attempt to persuade people to believe something, often by exaggeration or distortion of the truth.

Racial theory The belief that mankind is naturally divided into different races and that some races are superior to others.

Rani Indian title for a queen.

Repeal When Parliament abolishes a law.

Sans-culottes An eighteenth-century term for the poor people of Paris.

Scurvy A disease caused by lack of vitamin C.

Selective breeding When a farmer deliberately mates a male and female of different breeds to create offspring with desirable characteristics.

Sepoy An Indian word used to describe the Indian soldiers in the army of the British East India Company.

Suburbs The districts around the edge of a city or town, many newly built in the late nineteenth century.

Suffragettes The organisation that campaigned to win the vote for women before the First World War.

Suffragists Moderate campaigners for women's rights who did not believe in breaking the law and preferred persuasion rather than protest.

Taille A French word for a tax paid by all French peasants before the Revolution.

Tory The nickname for members of the Conservative Party.

Turnpike A barrier on a road designed to stop traffic so that a toll can be charged.

Tyrant A ruler who becomes oppressive to the people but cannot be challenged or replaced.

Ulster The region or province in the north of Ireland, most of which is still part of the United Kingdom.

Utilities Industries providing basic services such as water, gas and electricity.

Wall Street Crash When the values of shares sold on the US stock market fell very quickly in 1929.

Welfare State The attempt by the government to look after its citizens by providing pensions, education, health care and other benefits, all paid for out of taxation.

Zulus An African people living in modern South Africa.

Answers

Test your knowledge 1

1   a) Dr Malthus b) Jethro Tull c) 'Turnip' Townshend d) Samuel Crompton e) George Stephenson f) Isambard Kingdom Brunel g) Adam Smith h) Joseph Bazalgette i) Anthony Trollope j) Edward Jenner

2   a) Manchester b) Lancashire c) Rainhill d) City of London e) Lacock Abbey, Wiltshire f) Edinburgh g) London h) Crystal Palace, Hyde Park i) Crimean War j) America

3   a) 1801 b) 1801 c) 1828 d) 1825 e) 1815 f) 1846 g) 1858 h) 1870 i) 1840 j) 1848

Test your knowledge 2

1   a) Marie Antoinette b) Maximilien Robespierre c) Duke of Wellington d) Horatio Nelson e) Charles Darwin f) Charles and John Wesley g) Annie Besant h) Tolpuddle Martyrs i) Sir Robert Peel j) Elizabeth Garrett Anderson

2   a) 14 July 1789 b) January 1793 c) 1805 d) 1804 e) 1832 f) 1838 g) 1859 h) 1888 i) 1830 j) 1882

3   a) Tuileries Palace b) Varennes c) Corsica d) Russia e) Vienna f) Old Sarum g) Newgate Prison h) Crimean War i) Jamaica j) America

Test your knowledge 3

1   a) George III b) George Washington c) Sir Joseph Banks d) Fletcher Christian e) Captain Fitzroy f) Wolfe Tone g) William Wilberforce h) Olaudah Equiano i) Henry Morton Stanley j) Cetewayo

2   a) 1773 b) 1783 c) 1779 d) 1846 e) 1829 f) 1857 g) 1876 h) 1807 i) 1899 j) 1879

3   a) Paris b) Galapagos Islands c) Chile and Peru d) Ireland e) Mysore, in India f) Calcutta g) Isandhlwana h) Cape Colony i) Mafeking j) Brazil

Test your knowledge 4

1   a) Lord Reith b) Mussolini c) Franco d) Emmeline Pankhurst e) Margaret Thatcher f) Winston Churchill g) General Haig h) George V i) Lady Astor j) David Lloyd George

2   a) 1922 b) 1936 c) 1933 d) 1926 e) 1936 f) 1918 g) 1916 h) 1916 i) 1940 j) 1944

3   a) London b) Soviet Union c) Glasgow d) Dublin e) Dunkirk f) Epsom, the Derby race g) El Alamein h) Palace of Westminster i) Gallipoli in Turkey j) Russia

Countries of the British Empire

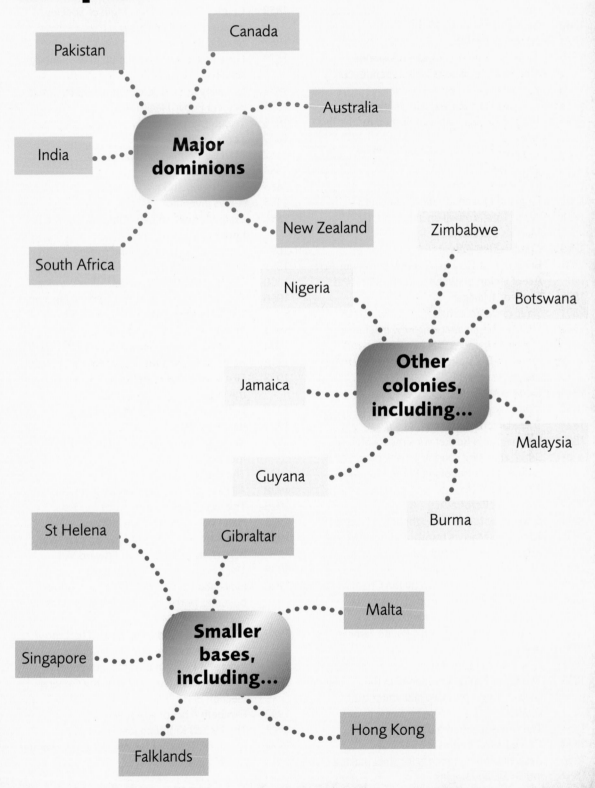

Major dominions
- Pakistan
- Canada
- Australia
- India
- New Zealand
- South Africa

Other colonies, including...
- Zimbabwe
- Botswana
- Nigeria
- Jamaica
- Malaysia
- Guyana
- Burma

Smaller bases, including...
- St Helena
- Gibraltar
- Malta
- Singapore
- Hong Kong
- Falklands

Timeline

1757	Battle of Plassey, the British begin to conquer India
1760	George III becomes King
1773	Boston Tea Party
1776	Adam Smith's *The Wealth of Nations*; American Declaration of Independence
1779	Captain Cook killed in Hawaii
1783	Treaty of Paris makes USA independent
1785	*The Times* newspaper published for the first time
1789	The French Revolution begins; The Mutiny on the Bounty
1792	Revolutionary Wars
1793	King and Queen of France executed
1798	Wolfe Tone's rebellion in Ireland; Dr Malthus's predictions
1799	Combination Acts
1801	Britain's first Census; General Enclosure Act; Act of Union between Britain and Ireland
1805	Battle of Trafalgar
1807	Slave trade abolished
1811	Luddites begin attacking new machines
1812	Napoleon invades Russia
1813	Elizabeth Fry's campaign for prison reform begins
1815	Battle of Waterloo
1817	Stethoscope invented
1824	Trade Unions legalised
1829	Stephenson's Rocket wins the Rainhill Trials; Burke and Hare caught; Emancipation of Catholics; Metropolitan Police founded
1830	The Swing Riots
1832	The Great Reform Act
1833	Slavery abolished throughout the Empire
1834	Tolpuddle Martyrs transported to Australia; Palace of Westminster burned down
1837	Victoria becomes Queen
1838	Great Charter drawn up by the Chartists
1840	Postage stamps introduced
1841	Photograph negatives invented
1846	Corn Laws repealed; Irish Potato Famine begins
1848	First Public Health Act
1851	The Great Exhibition opened at the Crystal Palace; telegraph cable laid under the Channel
1853	The cause of cholera discovered
1854	Crimean War begins
1856	Bessemer's new process for steel-making
1857	Indian Mutiny begins
1858	The Great Stink in London
1859	Charles Darwin's *The Origin of Species*; Samuel Smiles' *Self Help*
1867	Second Reform Act
1870	Local councils allowed to build elementary schools
1871	Dr Livingstone discovered in Ujiji by Stanley
1875	Second Public Health Act
1876	Telephone invented
1879	The Zulu War
1882	Married Women's Property Act
1884	Third Reform Act
1888	Match-girls' strike
1895	X-rays invented
1896	*Daily Mail* newspaper published for the first time
1897	Queen Victoria's Diamond Jubilee
1899	Boer War begins
1900	The Labour Party founded
1906	The Liberal Party wins the General Election; Trade Disputes Act
1913	Emily Davison dies at the Derby
1914	First World War begins
1916	Battle of the Somme; Easter Rising in Dublin
1918	First World War ends; women over 30 given the vote
1919	First woman MP to sit in Parliament
1921	Irish Free State founded
1922	Mussolini becomes ruler of Italy; BBC founded
1926	The General Strike
1928	All men and women over 21 given the vote
1929	The Wall Street Crash
1933	Hitler becomes ruler of Germany
1936	The Jarrow March; the Spanish Civil War begins; the abdication of Edward VIII
1939	The Second World War begins
1940	Evacuation at Dunkirk; Winston Churchill becomes prime minister; The Blitz begins over London
1945	The Second World War ends; The Labour Party wins the General Election
1947	India and Pakistan become independent
1951	The Conservative Party wins the General Election
1952	Elizabeth II becomes Queen
1973	The United Kingdom joins the EEC
1979	Margaret Thatcher becomes the first woman prime minister

Important prime ministers 1750-2000

1766–68 William Pitt the Elder – the politician who master-minded Britain's victories in the Seven Years War, when Britain conquered Canada in North America and Bengal in India

1770–82 Lord North – partly responsible for the start of the American War of Independence; blamed for many of the mistakes in the war

1783–1801 and 1804–06 William Pitt the Younger – Britain's leader during the early Napoleonic Wars, he introduced income tax to pay for the wars and harsh laws to deal with any possible revolution in Britain or Ireland

1806–07 Lord Grenville – abolished the slave trade in 1807

1830–34 Earl Grey – introduced the Great Reform Act in 1832

1834–35 and 1841–46 Robert Peel – invented the Metropolitan Police; tried to help with the Irish Potato Famine and repealed the Corn Laws

1868 and 1874–80 Benjamin Disraeli – introduced the Second Reform Act, claimed much of Africa for the British Empire and reorganised the Conservative Party

1868–74, 1880–85 and 1892–94 William Gladstone – introduced the Third Reform Act, reformed many aspects of how government worked and tried to give Home Rule to Ireland

1916–22 David Lloyd George – led Britain to victory in the First World War and agreed to southern Ireland becoming independent

1923–24, 1924–29 and 1935–37 Stanley Baldwin – led Britain through the crises of the General Strike and the Abdication of King Edward VIII

1924 and 1929–35 James Ramsay Macdonald – the first Labour prime minister and Britain's leader through the economic problems of the Great Depression

1940–45 and 1951–55 Sir Winston Churchill – Britain's inspiring leader during the Second World War

1945–51 Clement Attlee – the Labour leader who introduced the Welfare State

1979–90 Margaret Thatcher – the first woman prime minister; made radical changes to Britain's economy